Also Available

Shaking the Tree: brazen. short. memoir. Volume I

*Shaking the Tree: brazen. short. memoir. Volume II
(Things We Don't Talk About)*

Dear Melanie —   11/7/21
     Thanks for coming to my reading.
In looking forward to more fun w/ the
pickleball, theater, Trojan league,
dancing. We have so many common
interests!   ♡ Elise

shaking the tree

Vol. 3

I Didn't See That One Coming

Edited by Marni Freedman & Tracy J. Jones

Published by Memoir Writers Press
2801 B Street, #111
San Diego, CA 92102-2208
SDMWA.org

This book is a memoir anthology. It reflects the authors' present recollections of experiences over time. Some names and characteristics have been changed, some events may have been compressed, and dialogue may be recreated.

Copyedited by Erin Willard
Proofread by Stephanie Thompson
Book cover and interior design by Monkey C Media, www.monkeyCmedia.com

First Edition
Printed in the United States of America

ISBN (paperback): 978-0-9974413-2-1
ISBN (eBook): 978-0-9798551-7-7
Library of Congress Control Number: 2021916266

We want to dedicate this volume of
Shaking the Tree
to all of the first responders and front-line workers that so bravely stepped up during the onslaught of challenges that the last few years have brought to our doorsteps. To the health care workers, the police and firefighters, the truck drivers, the grocery workers, the childcare workers—-to anyone who got up and left the house while the rest of us hunkered down and stayed home, we see you. You put your life on the line and sacrificed day after day. We know you didn't see any of this coming, but once you did, you stepped up, and we are grateful.

Dear Reader,

We have a feeling you may relate to this year's theme: *I Didn't See That One Coming*. For all of us collectively, it's been that kind of year.

This volume is a unique collection that explores topics such as danger, coming of age, politics, affairs, survival, cults, abuse, wild sexuality, climbing mountains, and even the love of a pet chicken.

In the spirit of the *Shaking the Tree* series, this book goes there—unapologetically.

What we hope you get out of this, our third volume, is that everyone has a story—and by telling that story—they are letting you know how truly similar all of us are. In the end, when life throws us curveballs and pandemics, all we really have is each other.

Happy reading,

Marni and Tracy

Shaking the Tree, Vol. 3, 2021

brazen. short. memoir.

21 CANS

ELISE KIM PROSSER, PHD

April 1, 1981

I reached for the red can with the smiling Italian wearing a puffy white hat, Chef Boyardee. The hum of the electric opener, scrape of spoon against metal, smell of tin, heat from the stove, and tang of tomato sauce enveloping soft ravioli felt so familiar. Pretty tasty. Even after fourteen days in a row. Mommy had never allowed me to eat in front of the TV like this, but she'd been gone since the blue aerogram letter arrived two weeks ago.

Dear Daughter,

Mommy and I are going divorce.
She is too much independent.

Daddy.

I felt sucker-punched. I couldn't understand the rest of the letter, because it was written to Mommy in Korean. But you don't have to be bilingual to know your parents are fighting. Daddy had left us in America five years ago to teach in Korea, the country of his birth. I was born in Philadelphia and wanted to fit in, like any fifteen-year-old girl. I would've chosen a cheesesteak with peppers over bulgogi with kimchi. After Mommy read the letter, she packed her suitcase.

"I have to fly to Seoul tomorrow," Mommy explained. "Daddy got me a job interview at his university. Stay here, so you don't miss school. Tenth grade is important."

"Who's going to take care of me? My brothers?" Panic arose in my throat.

"No, they are busy at college."

"But I can't live alone." Tears rolled down my face.

"I'll be back in three weeks," she assured me.

Before she left, she opened the kitchen cabinet.

"I bought your favorite American food," she said. I stared at twenty-one cans of ravioli, for twenty-one days alone. Each can was like an X on the calendar until Mommy would return. Then she walked out the door, lugging her largest Samsonite. I sobbed on our shared bed, my Bonnie Bell lip gloss smearing the Holly Hobbie pillowcase. *How would I live by myself for three long weeks?*

Spying my American-history textbook, I remembered my upcoming test on the Declaration of Independence. My teacher stressed that it had been signed here in Philadelphia back in 1776. I looked up at my hero Rocky on a poster taped to the wall. I had stood in line for an hour to get an autograph from Sylvester Stallone. In my imagination, the strong boxer came alive. He urged me in his distinctive Philly accent: *Yo, get up off the mat.* Like him, I summoned the energy to rise and stamina to train. Studying all night, I felt determined to earn an A. Excellent grades were the only currency I earned that my parents valued.

Close to dawn, I crawled into bed for a few hours' sleep before catching the SEPTA bus to school. I missed the scent of Pond's Cold Cream Mommy used to apply before getting under the comforter in our bed in the tiny apartment. Shivering, I longed for her warm back snuggled against mine. With regret, I recalled the last time Mommy had nagged me. I retorted angrily: *Leave me alone!* Then she did . . .

Now Mommy's been gone fourteen days. Seven cans remained. I was really sick of ravioli. *Go the distance, just one more week,* I imagined Rocky coaching me. At least I received an A on my history test. I proudly tacked it on the refrigerator for Mommy to see next Wednesday. Every day, I had eagerly checked the mailbox for a letter with her arrival time. *Would she be waiting for me with a hug when I got home from school?*

My stained Eagles sweatshirt and wrinkled Jordache jeans stunk. I had run out of clean underwear. Without fresh food, I had diarrhea.

The garbage can in the kitchen overflowed. As I bent to pick up a discarded wrapper of butterscotch Tastykake, I saw a black cockroach against remnants of cream frosting. I shrieked with disgust, and the humongous bug scurried under the stove. I looked under the sink for Raid but did not find the insecticide. So, I took out the trash and rode my bike to Rite Aid. I broke my last ten-dollar bill on pest killer. I sprayed the linoleum until there was a puddle on the kitchen floor. The poisonous fumes made me feel nauseated. *I'm supposed to use the whole can, right?* Then I heard pounding at the front door.

"What is that terrible smell?" exclaimed Mrs. Hampel, the elderly tenant whose apartment was directly under ours.

"Sorry, it's Raid. I saw a roach."

She handed me a blue aerogram. "This letter was in my mailbox by mistake. And here's my rent check. Your Mom told me before she left to give it to you from now on." After Mrs. Hampel departed, I carefully scissored open the three sides along the red-and-navy border. *Why would Mommy tell her that?*

Dear Daughter,

I started the English professor job, so I can't return. Daddy and I live in a faculty housing and eat in the cafeteria, so I don't have to cook, shop, or commute. I can read and relax. We can't afford the private international high school for you, because we are paying college tuition for your brothers. Daddy says it's more important to invest in sons than a daughter. So stay in America where public high school is free. You must be independent. In Korea, the bank account is only in Daddy's name. The apartment quadplex in Philly is the only property in MY name. Collect rent from the three tenants, then pay mortgage and bills using my checkbook. Even though I miss you, be thankful for your good fortune.

Mom

The letter hit like a left hook I didn't see coming. My head spun and knees buckled. *Was this a cruel April Fools' joke?* Mommy must have known before she left that she would not return. I crushed her letter and threw it on the floor. I felt like the dying roach on its back, paralyzed with fear. My cries of anguish sounded like a wounded puppy whimpering for its mom. I felt like an orphan.

Sharp hunger pangs reminded me that I hadn't eaten all day, so I heated up my dwindling supply of ravioli. Six cans left. What would happen when I ran out of food? I ate in front of the TV, expecting to watch *The Facts of Life*, about teen girls at boarding school away from their parents. I fantasized about being nurtured by their house mother, Mrs. Garrett.

Darn, my favorite show wasn't on. Instead, there was news coverage of President Reagan, who had been shot by John Hinkley. The repeated scary images on TV made me feel vulnerable and afraid, stuck at home alone. Sitting crisscross applesauce on the shag carpet, it hit me: If the president of the United States wasn't safe, how could a fifteen-year-old girl be safe living alone?

***

April 1, 2020

Fast forward nearly forty years. Global pandemic COVID-19 has tragically killed 25,000 people. News and fake news are on 24/7. President Donald Trump assures Americans that the virus will miraculously be gone by Easter. *Is this another cruel April Fools' joke?* Dr. Fauci instructs us to "shelter in place" and work at home in order to "flatten the curve." To prepare, I run to the grocery store, wearing a mask and gloves, to stockpile food and supplies. Alarmed by the absence of toilet paper, disinfectant, and fresh food, I instinctively reach for the red can. At least Chef Boyardee is still smiling.

I open the kitchen cabinet and load canned goods. Sharp hunger pangs. The hum of the electric can opener, scrape of spoon against metal, smell of tin, heat from the stove, and tangy taste of tomato sauce enveloping soft ravioli felt so familiar. Even though I hadn't eaten it in almost forty years, the sounds, smell, and taste had lingered in my memory.

Mommy had never come back to take care of me. Twenty-one days had stretched to twenty-one months. I lived alone, subsisting on canned food for nearly two years during tenth and eleventh grade. After that, I had vowed never to eat canned food again. And I had kept that promise—until now.

While eating, I reread the blue aerograms found in a shoebox in Mother's closet after her recent funeral. *Dear Daughter.* The same feelings of fear, longing, and loneliness resurface. I reflect that April 1, 1981, ended my childhood and began my adulthood. It was a declaration of independence thrust upon me. Four decades later, in a rapidly spreading epidemic, people around the world realize that we are all interdependent.

I hear the key unlock the door.

"Mom, we're home," yells my son.

"We brought apple pie," adds my husband. Hugging them, my spirits soar.

"Yum. Lunch is ready." I serve them piping-hot ravioli.

"Pretty tasty," my son says with approval.

I take a deep breath.

"Did I ever tell you a story about this ravioli? I once had twenty-one cans . . ."

PHIL

CHILI CILCH

The Hostile Hospital. I held it in my hand and thought, this would be an amusing and suitable gift. It's the eighth book in the *Series of Unfortunate Events*, written by Lemony Snicket, aka Daniel Handler. I was at Costco, taking a late lunch, and had stopped to pick up flowers. Then I thought, check out the book section. In our few dates, I had learned that Phil liked to read. That scored him bonus points. Having a man, post-coitus, reading beside me, or even better, to me in bed, was my idea of hot.

Online dating was the new hookup mode. It was the year 2000, and I had just turned forty and was newly single, having ended my three-year relationship with Mark. Even though I was reluctant to sign up for Match.com, I kept hearing about friends of friends meeting their soul mates by the miracle of modern cyber matchmakers. It made some sort of sense. Getting to know the person by messaging a few times to decide if they might be worth the time and risk of a bad date. I know there are worse things, but thankfully I haven't experienced famine.

I cruised the pictures of my potential matches with sour dismay. I wasn't expecting George Clooney, but these men made no effort. I could've made a fortune if I had started a makeover business for these *boys* seeking women. I scrolled through pic after pic of men who took unflattering pictures under the fluorescent light of an office cubicle, or worse, in the bathroom mirror. A few friends accused me of being too picky, but I didn't think so. I figured the good-looking Joes were too much trouble, my criteria being men close to my age, ten years up or down, evidence of good hygiene, a nice smile, and the ability to spell most words. I was even willing to date a few inches shorter.

What really mattered to me was their ability to carry on a conversation. Not a common skill in my experience. If they were too quiet, I'd nervously end up talking about everything under the sun and revealing too much. I wasn't a sports girl, so that topic was off the table. I wanted to discuss all those taboo subjects; maybe not sex right off the bat, but politics and religion were my go-to subjects.

Phil made the first contact, and his message piqued my interest. He was witty and up on current events. I really should never date anyone unless they listen to NPR. After a few weeks of online flirting, we made a date midweek to get drinks after work. I suggested an English pub close to home. He was short and stocky, with thinning hair and glasses. But he possessed a confidence that I found attractive, and he made me laugh. Laughing is my aphrodisiac. We enjoyed an easy *When Harry Met Sally* banter.

We went on a few more dates, and I became increasingly hopeful that Match.com might be able to boast another cupid's arrow bull's-eye. I remember how excited he was to take me to his favorite Mexican restaurant so I could experience a pomegranate margarita. He was a foodie, politically liberal, we enjoyed the same music, and he was a decent kisser.

After the requisite three dates, I was interested in learning if we also shared some steamy sexual chemistry. I thought I would find out soon enough, thanks to California's farmworkers-rights activist César Chávez. We both had the next Monday free, the state holiday honoring Chávez. I was excited to spend the day with Phil, and if things went well, I'd be in my silky robe, kissing him goodbye later that evening. This would be the first time he was picking me up at my house, so I had to make sure the bed was made, and my home was presentable.

I showered, primped, and waited patiently. He didn't show. I texted, I called, I messaged on the dating site and got nothing—nada. I was pissed, then sad, then pissed again, so I likely got seriously pissed on booze later that evening. Or maybe I curled up in bed with a good book. I frankly can't remember.

What I do remember is going to work the next day. My cubicle mate, Carmen, couldn't wait to hear about my date. She was a good friend, a married pal that lived vicariously through my dating exploits.

"So, how was it?" she asked, the minute I sat down at my desk.

"He stood me up."

"No!"

"Yep, not even a text or phone call. He better be dead or in the hospital," I added.

Less than an hour later, my cell rang. It was Phil. "Hi, I'm so sorry, you're not going to believe this, but I'm in the hospital."

I pivoted in my office chair and mouthed to Carmen, "He's actually in the hospital." We're making these crazy dramatic faces at each other as I listened to Phil tell his story. He'd felt this incredible pain in his gut, unable to even walk, he was taken by ambulance to the hospital and rushed into emergency surgery for a gastrointestinal perforation.

"I just have one question, Phil, how the hell did you perforate your colon?" We laughed, and I asked, "Would you like me to come visit you?"

"Sure, that would be great, but let me call you back to make sure that I'll be here. They keep wheeling me away from my room for tests."

I hung up, and Carmen gave me a dubious look. "I'm calling the hospital." She did and confirmed he was there. Phil called me back, and I told him I'd be by to visit around two.

With Lemony Snicket's book in hand, I arrived at the hospital, ready to tease Phil about such a dramatic avoidance stunt to get out of our date. I asked the volunteer working the entrance for the room number. He wrote it down on a card for me. I took the elevator up to the sixth floor and found the room and peered in. I saw a white-haired couple sitting side by side against the wall and caught a wee glimpse of a third person standing at the head of the hospital bed. Umm, maybe that cute old guy volunteering in guest services gave me the wrong room number.

The hospital wing was strangely quiet; there were no nurses to inquire with. I wandered down the hallways, peeking furtively into other rooms. I paused again outside the room that was supposed to be Phil's. This time I caught a good look at the other person in the room. She suddenly turned and saw me lamely standing there.

"Can I help you?"

"I'm here to visit a friend, Phil, and I was told this is his room."

"Oh, hello," this attractive woman with long ginger hair greeted me, hand outstretched. "I'm Rosemary, Phil's wife."

I'm proud to say, I barely skipped a beat. "Hi, I'm Chili. I've heard so much about you." I stepped into the room and turned my head away from Rosemary to smile at Phil. "All good things, of course."

She clearly took me in with a bit of trepidation. "How do you know Chili, Phil?"

I have to appreciate that he was equally quick on his hospital-sock-footed feet. "Oh, she's friends with Judy, you know Judy, she works in my division." This was true; my friend Judy did work at his company. "We met at a work mixer."

This was a bald-faced lie. I looked at him, diminished, lying in a hospital bed in a faded blue smock. Instead of feeling pissed, I felt powerful. This man's marriage was at my mercy. I smiled again too broadly, giving Phil that *dude, you so owe me* look, and I made my visit brief. I cordially greeted his in-laws and somewhat substantiated Phil's story in a measly way to his wife. I handed over the book to Phil, saying, "This gift seemed appropriate, given your unfortunate circum-stances." He was too wrapped up in the enormity of our encounter.

I smiled, waved, turned on my heels toward the door, and made a graceful exit. *Wow*, I thought to myself. *Whatever gods, goddesses, might be at work and paying attention, good work.* I felt gratitude for dodging a bullet that would've wounded my tender heart, and I will always associate a perforated colon as a stunning example of the universe's power to bestow poetic justice.

THE INTERVIEW

KRISA BRUEMMER

Mom says I was her hardest kid. "The worst."

"You nearly drove me right up to the edge," Mom says.

I'm the oldest of three. My brother Josh crashed into a bus stop, drunk in the middle of the day, in our rural Washington town. My little sister Kaydi rode around without a helmet on the back of her decade-too-old boyfriend's motorcycle and told anyone who didn't like it to fuck right off. *But I was the worst.*

Mom was obsessed with Nordstrom—with appearances. I had expensive clothes, but we lived in a trailer at the edge of the woods. Mom warned us to stay in bed at night because rats snuck in. I'd fall asleep to the sound of her bitching and wake up to it again the next morning. It wasn't easy to get homework done or act normal in class. I always got good grades, though.

At sixteen, I pierced my nose with a safety pin, dyed my long hair bright green, and put on a six-dollar Goodwill dress. Mom said it was the ultimate insult. She *schemed* to keep me in brand-name clothes, selling food stamps for cash for Guess jeans, racking up thousands on Grandma's Nordstrom card so I'd have outfits that made rich girls' jealous.

How dare I shop at Goodwill?

Mom never stopped bitching about money. By the time I hit high school, she had started driving *me* up to the edge. We'd been kicked out of the trailer, and there were five of us crammed into a one-bedroom house.

"Hypocrite," I growled when Mom walked in, weighed down by Nordstrom bags.

"Who are you to judge my choices?" Mom yelled. "I only married your loser, son-of-a-bitch dad so you wouldn't have to be a bastard child, and ever since then, just about every second of every God-damned day has been fucked up and then some. I could've been a supermodel with a perfect life if it wasn't for you."

One day, Mom pushed me down the stairs, and shit hit the fan. She exploded when I told her to get off the phone so I could call my boyfriend, a punk rocker named Skeet; we only had one cordless in the house. Mom turned rabid within seconds, the corners of her mouth foaming as she threw the cordless at my face. When Mom shoved me and I tumbled down the stairs, her boyfriend held her back and told me to run.

I sprinted barefoot in the rain up a muddy hillside trail to my friend's house. The next morning, I snuck back in to get my backpack, and my friend Roxanne picked me up. When I called home from Roxanne's house, I expected Mom to say, "Get your ass home!" But she didn't.

"I'm beyond sick of your bullshit," Mom said. "Don't come back."

I stayed with Roxanne, bussed tables for five bucks an hour, did my homework, and gouged a scar deep into my arm with a pinecone for some reason I never understood, and then I lied about it, telling people I'd burned myself on the espresso machine at work. I wondered if I was technically a homeless kid. I couldn't imagine how I'd make it to college or out of our town at all if that was how I had to live day to day.

One night after a party, I lost control of my grandma's car. Looking out over the cliff I'd barely missed, my heartbeat was louder than the Nirvana blasting from the speakers. Mom had always warned me not to drink and drive, to turn the music down if it was dark.

Mom made everything so damn hard, like a ten-pound weight inside my backpack that no one could feel but me. I could've been a straight-A student *easy* if I'd had a different life. Instead, I was shaking and sobbing at the edge of a cliff, too caught up in the unfairness of it all to think straight.

And that's when it all became clear—I knew I didn't have it in me to make it another year in that small town. The next day, I went to the guidance counselor, Ms. Dorn, who I often visited to get out of class.

"Can you send me to England to study writing?" I asked. As far-fetched as it seemed, I wondered if Ms. Dorn could make it happen.

"How about drumming in Ghana?" she asked.

I didn't really want to leave Skeet and my friends, but I was panicking, worried that if I couldn't find an escape route right that minute, I'd end up stuck, trapped in a tiny town with Mom forever.

I hoped Ms. Dorn couldn't see through my fake smile as she handed me an American Field Services brochure with a picture of a happy host family in front of their mud hut in the desert. I hadn't talked to Mom in weeks, but showing Grandma that brochure got Mom to call.

"You've got another thing comin' if you think you're gallivanting off to who-the-fuck-knows where to live in a godforsaken mud hut," Mom screamed through the phone.

"You're so backwards!" I yelled back.

But I knew Mom was right. I wasn't interested in drums, and I'd never thought about Ghana.

"What about Italy?" Mom asked.

I hadn't seen that coming.

Italy was full, but Switzerland had room.

"I can't stay here next year, Mom. But for this to work, you have to go to the interview."

"Fine. But I'm not showing up with my kid looking like a green-haired freak show."

On the way to my interview, Mom and I discussed tactics.

"They wanna know if I can get along with a host family, so *we have to lie.*"

Mom glared and said, "You should have more confidence in me, Krisa."

Mom and I walked in, wearing carefully selected Nordstrom outfits, our makeup subtle Clinique. My hair had been cut into a dark-brown pixie. We met my interviewer, Heidi, with friendly handshakes and big smiles, but my voice shook. Mom looked perfect as she introduced herself.

"Tell me a bit about your home life," Heidi said. "How do you get along with your siblings? What are your household rules, and how are they enforced?"

I went blank. My brother had once nearly broken my nose. When I came downstairs gushing blood, Mom said, "You had it comin'. Go clean up the mess."

Mom put on her most confident *I should've been a supermodel* self. "Krisa has always been easy," Mom told Heidi. "She gets straight As, and her siblings adore her. If she studies abroad, we'll miss her every minute."

It felt like the earth had shifted, as if someone else had entered Mom's body and taken control, blasting me down a portal toward a potentially bright future. Mom looked at me and smiled, her eyes saying, "You're fuckin' welcome. Now turn it on."

"Mom has always been my biggest supporter," I said, cautiously. "She cheers the loudest at my track meets and rewards me for my grades."

"You work so hard, I wish I could give you more," Mom interrupted.

I kicked it up a notch, fueled by the realization that with Mom on my side, I could say anything.

"Mom has always worked hard for us. I like making dinner because Mom has a long commute. Most weekends, I babysit so that she can have a break." Heidi seemed impressed. "But I've made mistakes," I said, not wanting the sugar coating to get too heavy. "I backed Mom's car into a power pole."

"I was pretty upset that day," Mom said. "But it was an accident."

Mom told Heidi she'd grounded me for a month. She said I watched my siblings and cooked to make up for my mistake. The truth was I'd never cooked in my life. And I refused to babysit, preferring to spend my weekends with Skeet. For the next hour, Mom and I fed off each other's lies. The only honest things we said were about my grades.

"We pulled that off, didn't we?!" Mom said afterward.

"You should've been an actress," I said.

Mom looked the happiest I'd seen her in years.

We laughed the whole way home. But underneath my relief, there was panic. Mom and I were finally getting along, united against the system. But I had to go halfway around the world without her, to a place where I wouldn't even know how to talk, to escape the fucked-up situation *she'd* put me in.

After three nerve-wracking days, Heidi called. I was in.

"You have to go," Mom said. "Swiss chocolate is to die for!"

I returned home from Switzerland a year later, a new person who spoke a new language, a month away from attending an elite New England private university. I had earned over twenty-five thousand dollars in scholarships, and a grant would cover my tuition. But I knew I owed Mom everything.

Before I left for college, Mom told me she didn't think Swiss chocolate was all that.

"It's hardly even as good as Hershey's."

I agreed, but it was a lie. At the airport, I told her she was the best mom in the whole entire world. As her smile lit up and she hugged me goodbye, the truth didn't matter. I was free.

ELEPHANT IN THE ROOM

KENNY SUCHER

I felt the rage rising in my body like bass from a speaker growing louder and louder. Talking to him was like talking into a black hole. We stood red face to red face in his living room. Everything I tried to explain to him seemed to come back to me as infuriatingly pointless off-topic questions. Like trying to flush a clogged toilet without a plunger, it just kept getting worse. I probably should have known better, but I thought I could handle this. Handle him.

He was blue-eyed and preppy, his teeth so white I'd keep a running tally of compliments he received about them. He wore out-of-fashion shoes and ill-fitting jeans, but I love a project. He had recently finished med school, and my friends would start eventually referring to him as "the Doctor."

I was in my thirties, rafting through the rough dating waters of self-important DC gay boys, having been dumped recently by one of them. The culprit sat me down, after a relatively stress-free eight months of dating, and told me that after discussing our relationship with his therapist, he didn't see a future with me.

"I just need someone with more drive, professionally," he said, very matter-of-factly, like stabbing someone in the gut with a smile.

I mentioned my master's degree to him and other resume-worthy accomplishments as if he were an HR recruiter, attempting to convince him, and me, of my worth. I handed him a small box of his things, and he left.

Dating was starting to feel like a game of dodgeball, hoping you weren't the last to be picked, then desperately trying to avoid getting hurt, soon finding yourself nursing a wound from a hit you never saw coming. It just seemed safer to stay on the sidelines. I always hated sports anyway. When I was younger, my father pushed me to play, but once he saw how I threw a ball, he dumped me too, focusing his attention on my brother's burgeoning wrestling career instead. I guess I lacked drive in that department as well.

So, I started off cautiously with the Doctor, like handling something just out of the oven, trying my best not to get burned. And after a few months, I started to let my guard down. Looking back, though, I realized there were obvious red flags I'd overlooked. Jealousy over my friends, overreacting to perceived slights. And the time he snatched his hand away when I tried to hold it in public. "Someone could see us," he said. But I tended to ignore the flaws of guys I dated, since I was usually busy worrying about my own.

Back in his living room, we stood in silence, gritting our teeth. I figured saying anything at this point would be worthless, so I silently began to glance around the room instead. I noticed his dusty fake bamboo plant sitting atop his espresso-colored coffee table surrounded by a gray sofa accented with slightly darker-toned throw pillows. On his wall, a framed sketch of his alma mater hung next to a blue-and-white collegiate flag. It was nice enough décor, with a few missteps, like something out of a Rooms-To-Go showroom that was targeted toward former frat boys. Inoffensive, masculine, and handsome, just like its owner. Yet it was furnishing that hid some probable instability and bad construction underneath, also like its owner. But we were gay men. Instability and bad construction were traits we were supposed to wear proudly, like badges of honor, but he wasn't there yet.

I finally muttered at him, "Stupid."

"Are you calling me stupid?" he asked.

"No," I replied, "but your opinion is stupid."

I wanted to make this work, since he seemed so perfect at the start. I mean, he fit so many of my prerequisites. He was age-appropriate, good-looking, and charming, a professional. He was a doctor, for Christ's sake, which even fit my mom's prerequisites. But the catch, because there's always a catch, was that he was a Republican. A gay Republican, like an agnostic priest; it just didn't make sense to me. And when I found out, I figured it would be a problem, but it was a problem, like his fashion sense, that I thought I could fix.

I had gotten pretty good at dealing with problems in my relationships. It was easier to focus on a solution than dwell on why I stayed. For example, I once used a calendar to track the moods of a possibly bipolar ex-boyfriend, and I gifted Klonopin to a socially anxious one. I used to trick another possibly alcoholic ex into drinking water by adding a lime and stir-straw to the glass to make it look like a cocktail. He was usually too drunk to tell the difference. Maybe it was all the water that I tricked him into drinking that caused him to wet the bed occasionally, but I just bought a plastic mattress cover to take care of that. Hell, I even had a bag full of tricks, many years ago, to deal with my experimental ex-girlfriends who were always suspicious about my lack of interest in bed.

It seemed best, in this situation, to just avoid the topic of politics altogether. And that worked for a bit, but it finally came up one night when he demanded to watch his favorite politician give a speech.

"I'm into politics," he explained. But he said "politics" the same way the nuns in grade school used to use the word "religion" to refer to Catholicism. We attempted to watch the speech together. I refuted some of the claims. He came back at me. It started politely at first, but it was still an argument, a political argument. And those are hard to win or lose. You reference a fact, the other disputes the source. It's just an endless cycle where no one wins and no one surrenders, like two fighting betta fish in a bowl. Luckily though, in this case, we found an out.

"*Your* opinion is stupid," he responded, "and your arm looks really good in that T-shirt with your stupid opinions."

I started to blush. "Well, you're the one who wanted to watch this stupid debate with your pretty blue eyes and your stupid sexy face."

Politics suddenly took a backseat, and we started kissing somewhere around that point. The kissing led to his bedroom for some make-up sex fueled by conflicting emotions of love and hate—really the best kind. And like so many couples before us, it was much easier just to enjoy the moment than worry about what would happen after our honeymoon phase ended.

After we exited the bedroom, I began checking my phone, and he went to the fridge to grab a beer, cracking it open as he sat down on his sofa. He switched the channel to ESPN as a probable compromise. He soon began shouting again, but this time it was at some baseball or football team of his that was losing. He took another sip of beer, put his legs up on the coffee table, and asked me to move a little more to the right since I was blocking his view. *Oh shit*, I thought. I'm not just dating a Republican. I'm dating my father.

IT'S JUST A PAIR OF GLASSES

LAURA L. ENGEL

June 1968.

"You didn't wait up." My husband Nick lunged toward me in the tiny apartment. Startled out of a deep sleep, my heart pounded hard as my baby rolled inside of me, sending a vigorous kick to my side.

***

It was a warm, humid evening on the Mississippi Gulf Coast. Not even a slight breeze rustled through the oak trees. I had opened all the windows, and our ancient fan turned slowly. Looking out from my second-story window, I saw the night was pitch black. The only light in the neighborhood was the dim one hanging precariously over our front door. Nick wanted me to wait up for him. He made me promise I would.

I was six months pregnant and dead tired after working at my meager-paying child-care job. My swollen feet ached and my back throbbed. Plus, I faced another early day tomorrow. All I wanted was to fall into bed and sleep forever.

Almost midnight. Where is he?

The sixteen-inch black-and-white TV was turned low. I sat slowly rubbing ice cubes up and down my arms, watching Walter Cronkite talking about the recent Bobby Kennedy assassination on the tiny screen. Changing the channel, I saw a commercial by Clairol for a new hair product, Summer Blonde, promising you'd have more fun if you simply bleached your hair. I quickly switched the channel again and was staring at the faces of young soldiers who had died that week in the war.

Nick still has a year to serve. What if he's sent to Vietnam?

I glanced at the red plastic clock on the wall.

Past midnight.

Nick had probably stopped after work for beers with his friends, young army guys, all far from home. He couldn't expect me to wait up all night. Could he?

It felt heavenly snuggling under the soft, laundered sheets, and almost immediately, I fell into a glorious deep sleep. But within minutes, I jerked awake, sensing his presence before I saw him.

"Why'd you go to bed?" he sneered, grabbing at the bedpost to steady himself. I heard the familiar, unmistakable pent-up rage in his voice and I immediately sat up, yanking the tangled sheet off my ballooning middle, and grabbed for my glasses.

"You're supposed to wait up, Laura. You promised you always would," he whined, as he stumbled back into the kitchen, opened the fridge, and rummaged for beer. I flinched when I heard a chair tip over with a deafening bang.

Entering the living room, I made a wide circle around him. As I sat down on our Goodwill sofa, I snuggled into the pillows and smoothed my cotton nightgown across my belly.

"Did you have fun?" I tried to smile through my exhaustion. There were only a few hours before I had to leave the house for my babysitting job. We needed that extra money.

Nick grumbled and settled into his favorite spot on the couch, ignoring my question and popping open his beer, which slopped out of the can as he shook off his uniform. I cringed as the alcohol spilled onto the rug. A strong smell of yeast filled the air. He slammed the beer down onto a stack of newspapers. I watched it tipping to the side, forcing myself not to reach out and straighten it as his cigarette smoke filled the room.

I sat silent.

I had never known another human being like Nick—self-absorbed, twenty-one, ready to boil over any minute. After six months of marriage, I was determined not to get him going. I had learned the hard way what happened when I spoke my mind.

Once, when I complained the trash can was overflowing, he hurled it out of our second-story window and left a mountain of trash for me to pick up. My cheeks burned as I remembered the neighbors' faces.

He'd also punched a couple of holes in the walls. I'd covered those gashes with posters of the Beatles' *Magical Mystery Tour*.

He often told me that he had lost his cool because I was such a nag, adding, "You're lucky I never hit you."

Slouched in his corner, face flushed, belly stuck out, he resembled a pouting infant. He glared at me.

I hope our baby is nothing like him. Jekyll and Hyde.

Just then, my baby gave another powerful kick. I chuckled softly.

"What's so funny?"

"The baby just kicked." I rubbed my stomach, grinning at him.

"Liar. You were looking at me when you laughed. You laughed at me."

"God, Nick, you think everything is about you."

The second I said it, I knew it was the wrong thing to say. I quickly smiled, ready to apologize as his face darkened. My heart and head pounded; my throat closed.

Oh, God. What did I just do?

He lunged toward me with his hand raised. His slap hit my face with such force, my neck made a cracking sound. My glasses flew from my face, breaking and slicing across my nose and cheek. Instant pain was followed by shock as they sailed across the room.

"Don't ever laugh at me, you stupid, stupid bitch!" he screamed, his face inches from mine.

I rolled in a ball and sobbed, my arms instinctively protecting my middle. Bloody drool filled my mouth from a split lip, and I wiped it as it ran onto my chin.

Crawling on my hands and knees, uncontrollable keening sounds coming from somewhere deep inside of me, I gathered up the pieces of my glasses with shaking hands.

The frames were broken, and the lens shattered. Gagging, afraid I would vomit, I cowered as Nick stood above me, fists clenched. I knew I would pay for this, and I began repeating, "I'm sorry. I'm sorry."

After a momentary standoff, he turned and stumbled toward the bedroom, grumbling, "We can't afford new glasses." He slammed the bedroom door, then yelled, "Get your parents to buy you new ones."

I can't see a thing without my glasses, and how can I explain my cut face to Mama and Daddy?

I held my bloody face over the kitchen sink, cautiously dabbing a wet dishcloth over my cheekbone and nose, afraid to enter the bedroom where Nick lay passed out, snoring.

Where will I find money for new glasses?

My body ached all over, but worst of all, my baby was still, as if afraid of making its presence known.

Please let my baby be okay.

Spending a sleepless night on the couch, I held a cold cloth on my torn cheek, trying to think up excuses for my ravaged face.

How did I get here?

My mind circled in a continuous loop. Exactly a year ago, I had been hidden away in an unwed-mothers' home. With no man to marry me and no way to support the child, my parents had insisted I relinquish my newborn son for adoption. Forbidden to speak of my experience once I returned home, I had lived in my private hell, secretly mourning that baby. When Nick asked me to marry him, I had jumped at the chance to escape the shame of my old life, with hopes of having another child as quickly as possible.

My world was blurry as I looked around the cramped living room, the pillows I had sewn, the secondhand furniture I had painted, and the framed black-and-white photo of Nick and me smiling on our wedding day.

***

Watching the early morning sunlight filter through the windows, my mind shifted. There were no tears left to cry. I wrapped my arms around my middle, cradling my precious unborn child, and rose, unsteady on my feet. Tiptoeing into the kitchen, I prepared the morning coffee just the way Nick liked it, piping hot, strong, and black. I placed the eggs and bread on the counter, deciding to make French toast, his favorite. And this is what I told myself:

Nick knew about my past and still married me.

He has a good job.

I shouldn't have laughed.

It's just a pair of glasses.

THE WINDS OF KILIMANJARO

ELIZABETH ESHOO

I am fully clothed, layered in long underwear, thermal socks, a turtleneck, a fleece jacket and pants, a down vest, and a wool hat and gloves, and zipped snugly into my minus-twenty-degree sleeping bag at 15,500 feet on the rocky slope of Mt. Kilimanjaro under a spectacularly bright full moon. I am just eight hours away from realizing my dream.

Lying next to me are my three tentmates, and we are all struggling to breathe at this altitude. I hear Dennis tossing and turning and notice he is still wearing the beaded choker he traded with the Maasai warrior over a week ago. Not far from us, another fellow climber is coughing relentlessly to rid his lungs of fluid and is dangerously close to having pulmonary edema. My heart keeps skipping beats. I can't tell if I've slept at all, but at midnight, we'll be roused to get ready for the final ascent to the summit at 19,341 feet. After nearly a week on this mountain, it's hard to believe we'll finally be at the peak, above the clouds, next to the ancient glacier, and sitting atop the highest mountain on the continent.

I've come so far to be here. I don't mean "from the base of this mountain" far. I mean "from a childhood dream of one day coming to Africa" far. Movies like *Born Free* and *Out of Africa* and books like *West with the Wind* and everything Hemingway wrote about Africa painted a picture of fascinating people, wild landscape, and adventure that stood in stark contrast to my suburban upbringing. It took a cancer scare and a cheating boyfriend to get me thinking that at age twenty-eight, it was the right time to come. As if those life-changing setbacks weren't challenging enough, I blew out my knee while running in Nairobi on day one. Day. One.

A week after the knee injury, on the eve of the climb, I crumbled to the red Tanzanian dirt in full-body aches and a fever of 104 that stole away my strength and almost my chance to climb—but not my will. I came to Africa to heal my wounded heart and womb, but also to find an expanded version of myself, one that would carry me through life with a deep sense of purpose and self-knowing. And, of course, I came to claim victory at the top of this mountain.

When I hear the echo of the wake-up bell, I roll over to unzip my sleeping bag and feel a sharp stabbing pain in my knee. I could swear there is an ice pick wedged between my kneecap and the lower outside joint of my left knee. I sit up too quickly and become dizzy. I remind myself to move "*polepole*," —slowly, as the Swahili mantra warns, advice we've been trying to follow with every step we've taken so far on this mountain.

NN, our capable Tanzanian guide, is barely bigger than the overstuffed pack he is carrying on his back. I wonder why it's so large when mine holds nothing more than a bottle of water and my camera. His usual expressive smile is obscured by the darkness of the hour and, at times, absent altogether due to the seriousness of the task at hand. He directs our group of ten hikers to form a single-file line. I am in the lead, as the rule on the mountain is to hike as fast as the slowest hiker. That has been me this entire journey. While the group gets organized, I reach into my pocket for an extra hand warmer and instead pull out the feather that NN gave me the first day of the climb. He told me his Chagga people believe feathers carry the spirit of the Kibo god.

"It will help you fly up the mountain," he had assured me.

NN and his patient guidance, his unwavering belief in me, and perhaps the power his feather imparted, have helped me every step of the past four days as I struggled to overcome the fatigue from the Rift Valley fever, the excruciating pain in my knee, and the nausea that set in at 13,500 feet. Despite the subzero temperature and the sleepless night, I feel energized by the challenge ahead and confident my own spirit will carry me to the top. But I tuck the feather back into my pocket, just in case.

The switchback trail is steep and covered in a slippery layer of pebbles, but the group of us soon falls into a rhythmic rest step that we've been practicing all week on this climb, moving in unison as we snake our way up to the top. There are no trail markers, barely a path, just the inky blackness of the night in front of me, as the light of the full moon stays put in the sky. With every blind step I take, I have to trust this mountain, this journey into the unknown. I take one step and then four breaths. I take another step, and my foot slides back under the loose scree. I lose ground. It's like climbing a vertical beach. This is nothing like I imagined while training on the Stairmaster in my hiking boots and a weighted backpack at my Upper East Side gym.

I lose track of time. I lose track of my pain. All I can think about is the next step and the next breath. One step. Four more breaths. I possess a laser focus that propels me onward; it feels like I could hike forever. I realize that I am capable of doing anything if I put my mind to it. I know the can-do overachiever mindset, the one that helped me accumulate A's in school, trophies from tennis championships, and promotions at work. But this mindset is different. I am overwhelmed by this brief glimpse of a new inner power and feel an upwelling of chills tingling throughout my entire body.

Standing alone on the lunar-like landscape—I mean really alone, with no light, no air, no water, no trees or plants or critters of any kind, and my fellow climbers so far behind—I feel like a stranger to myself. Nothing that makes me successful in my career or my life in New York City will help me in this moment. My former self seems a universe away from the woman standing here on the mountainside.

I feel a deep sense of loneliness. Despite being with a close-knit group of climbers, we are alone with our thoughts, our bodily struggles, and the overwhelming reality that while we are all heading to the summit, we each take our unique journey to get there. Each step, our own. I feel relief when the group catches up to me, and we gather in a tight circle, our arms reaching out to form a group hug.

An enormous orange orb peeks over the black horizon line and lights up the narrow trail ahead of us. With light, there's hope and a renewed source of energy from within when I see the sign ahead and realize I will make it to this first summit at 18,640 feet. The highest point, Uhuru Peak, is just 700 feet farther.

"Six and a half hours to Gillman's Point. That's record time," NN tells us, with a giant smile and no sign of fatigue.

A deep level of self-satisfaction and gratitude for being with my fellow climbers washes over me as we all revel in our accomplishments with high-fives and hugs. I rub my knee and feel grateful I've made it this far.

Kilimanjaro makes its own weather, and it has decided to whip up gale-force winds. The bliss of our peak moment fades instantly when a sudden gust of worry sweeps over the group sitting there on the rocky ledge at Gillman's. What had been annoying symptoms of acute mountain sickness for most of us unexpectedly turn life-threatening for Dennis in a matter of seconds. "He has no pulse!" "Dennis is dead!" Our oxygen-deprived brains sputter a slew of untruths until we see Dennis get into a sleeping bag that NN pulls out of his oversized backpack to reverse Dennis's hypothermia. But one truth remains: people die on Kilimanjaro.

NN and the other guides quickly assemble our group into two new patrols: those proceeding up to Uhuru and those returning to base camp. "We need to get going to the summit, now!" NN says, his easygoing demeanor transformed into a seriousness I hadn't seen before.

I study the trail ahead and see the outer edge of the jagged glacier wall, obscuring the coveted peak, but I can feel it. I can feel the moment I stand arm-in-arm with my fellow climbers and snap a photo I'll hang in my office. I can't wait to tell the story of victory to everyone back home. My feet automatically move toward the group going to Uhuru when NN walks up to me and says, "I want you to head down the mountain."

"No!" I blurt. "I'm fine, NN." With the threat of losing my opportunity to summit, I feel a boost of adrenaline replenish my energy reserves. "It's only 700 more feet."

"It will take you at least two more hours to get to Uhuru. Then at least three to get back down to base camp, and even longer if we decide to go to a lower altitude tonight. I am worried for your knee," NN says, his eyes burrowing into mine.

A wave of disbelief and disappointment blows through my entire being. His words do more to weaken my knees than the arduous hours of climbing. *How can this be happening?* I think of all the planning, training, preparation, and dreaming about this very moment, and I walk over to the Uhuru group just to prove him wrong. He follows me and puts his compact little body between the climbers going to the summit and me.

"Hiking down is the most dangerous part of the climb and going down will be so much more painful for you."

Not more than missing my chance to summit. Doesn't he get how strong I am? I know I can do this; I know I can summit. A gust of wind draws my glance back to Dennis, and the group of climbers still working to revive him, and then I look into NN's eyes. I see a world of worry in them for me, and I know at this moment, I must put my trust in his wisdom, as I have done every step of the way so far. I take one last look toward the summit as I let NN's cautionary words soak in, *polepole.* "Okay," I say.

Standing on the roof of Africa, I look out over the massive panoramic view and watch as a graceful bird soars through the butterscotch sky. I'm reminded of NN's feather, and also the warning we learned on the first night of this journey: Expect the unexpected while in Africa. This is not what I expected, but I wonder, *what happens if I let go of expectations?* And then, I feel the winds of Kilimanjaro shift again. I am surprised when a cool breeze of *contentment* washes over me. I head back down the mountain, leaving nothing but deep satisfaction in my wake.

THE VISIT

NICOLA RANSON

I had long suspected that my father didn't love me. At twenty-four, I had proof: a two-finger-typed letter mailed across the continent from my parents' home near Montreal. It was 1981. The paper was singed with Papa's white-hot words: "No daughter of *ours* could behave as you have done." That sentence sliced open my guts. Untethered, I floated in disbelief. *Was he cutting me off?* Later I learned that I'd been excised from their will. By then, the wound had blistered into fury: How dare he deny I was their daughter! My mother's words were equally shocking. She reversed her life's beliefs and said on the phone, "We should have taken you to church."

"But Mummy, you don't believe in God; why would you have done that?"

I knew why. Because this thing I'd done was so awful: I'd fallen in love. Not with a regular man, or a woman (even that would've been better). I'd fallen for a guru. In 1979, when I'd sat in the hot, humid hall in India and heard Bhagwan Shree Rajneesh's sweet voice, my heart cracked open. When I was initiated, he looked me in the eyes, and I felt completely seen. When he touched my forehead, my body crumpled to the marble floor while I traveled to a far-off planet of extraordinary bliss, as if God's breath had graced my cheek. After that, there was no choice; I had a tremendous thirst to be with Bhagwan and the others who understood. My parents saw us as a group of zombies wearing orange. I saw an array of diverse and creative people who all happened to have fallen in love with the same man.

In 1981, Rajneesh left India for the United States to live on a hundred square miles of sagebrush in Oregon's remote backcountry. This became the commune we called the Ranch. By 1984, I'd been living there for three years and hadn't seen my parents in four.

"Nicola, when are you coming home?" Their letters enclosed press clippings calling my group a cult. It was like opening a package of darts. My father was a domineering man who'd once said all priests should be shot. I wrote back: "This *is* my home. And please call me by my name. I'm not Nicola anymore. I'm Pyari."

I'd heard that some parents kidnapped their children and forced them into deprogramming. Would mine do that? I didn't want to visit them. I'd had it with their harsh, critical world, but I still missed them and longed for them to enter mine.

"Come and see me! We've built a hotel for our city—with round beds. Prem sends his love." Prem was my husband of three years. They'd never met him.

"We certainly won't. No money of ours is going to the Bagwash." That's what Papa called my guru, as if the actual name would soil his mouth.

What I didn't tell them was that I couldn't have visited them even if I'd wanted to. If I'd left the Ranch of my own accord, there was no guarantee of return, a separation which would have felt like death. Besides, I didn't have any money. It was hard enough to buy a postage stamp. Calling was even more difficult. I had to skip dinner to get to the building with the phones before the queue was too long. I called when I could:

"I've got news. We're offering a three-day visit for parents, free of charge."

"How generous." I was used to my mother's dismissive disdain—and was shocked when, weeks later, I received a letter saying that they'd decided to make the three-thousand-mile trip to the Ranch, which was a long way from anywhere. Perhaps they did miss me?

When the Ranch bus arrived from Portland, I was called to the Visitors' Center. My heart filled with hope that, in the commune's magical atmosphere, we could connect at last. Everyone from the bus was wearing orange except for the two figures standing side by side in their brown clothes, smaller than I remembered. We hugged clumsily, like strangers.

"I'll take you to your A-frame. We built them from tent platforms."

My parents were eerily polite. They even liked their room.

"It's very nice. And clean. With a private bathroom," said my mother. What had she expected?

"How are things at home?"

"Your mother has redone our bathroom. With pink wallpaper."

I felt like I was entertaining people from outer space. Once bathroom renovations were exhausted, what else could we talk about? I'd heard no outside news in three years.

Introducing Prem was weird. They all shook hands politely.

"I understand you work in computers," said Papa. "That's lucrative."

"Could be, but I gave all my money to the commune."

"Well, we're very happy you two have one another," said my mother.

"We're so lucky, aren't we?" Prem squeezed my shoulder, making me cringe. I changed the subject.

"When is your Ranch tour tomorrow? My coordinator gave me time off."

"That's big of her to spare you from pricing plumbing parts," said my mother. I let it slide.

The next day, the Twinkie (our name for the tour hostess) driving the minibus rattled on about our accomplishments. Our environmental improvements were significant, but we'd have built Bhagwan a coal-powered shoe factory if that's what he'd wanted.

"And where does the—er, Bhagwan live?" Papa spat out the name.

"We're unable to tell you, for security reasons," gushed the Twinkie. I had to wrap my index finger in my other hand to counter my desire to point toward his house. Even worse was not being able to show them my home. "That's our trailer over there. Sorry, we can't ask you in. It's for the privacy of the other four residents." Twelve, more like. I had to give the number that met our zoning restrictions. All this doublespeak was making me nauseated.

The next day, my parents were taken to a lecture at the Visitors' Center. When we met for lunch, Papa had brightened considerably.

"I found out that you can own private property. You and Prem could open your own business. He could use his computer skills." Apparently, my skills were invisible.

"I've never thought about it," I mumbled. I was astonished at the creativity of the PR department—was this a setup for a parental investment? How could I burst Papa's bubble and say it was utter nonsense? The Ranch had achieved a small miracle by getting him more relaxed and positive.

"Finish up your salads. We don't want to be late," I said. At last, I could show my parents the reason I was there, by taking them to the guru's daily drive-by. We lined up alongside two or three thousand residents and visitors waiting for Bhagwan to cruise by in one of his Rolls-Royces. I was flooded with happiness and hoped my parents would feel the contagious joy. I took Papa's camera, in case Bhagwan stopped and looked at them with his deep brown eyes. "He's coming, he's coming!" An expectant hush pulsated along the ribbon of orange, now silent except for clusters with guitars singing love songs. My parents stood obediently still as the car passed slowly by.

The following year, after the Ranch had ended, I felt sympathy when I looked at the photo of their flat, void faces reflected in the shiny paint on the Rolls. At the time, I imagined—were they beginning to open up? I longed for some softening. That happened for one glorious moment the next day, October 13, my mother's birthday. I'd organized a cake in the restaurant and told the French waitress my mother was part French. As Mummy blew out the candles, the staff sang her an old French folk song. The orange patrons all around us cheered, and I brimmed with pride—my Ranch people knew how to celebrate!

"Thank you, *merci*." Teared up and flustered, Mummy brandished the cake knife, then did something extraordinary. She turned toward the nearby disciples and offered them slices of cake. My mother had reached out—to the orange enemy! But a slice of cake later, the stilted conversations returned.

Prem was a lifesaver when we debriefed that evening. "How are you holding up?"

"It's the longest three days of my life. They're so closed down." I was shocked by the next words out of my mouth: "I wouldn't be surprised if I never saw them again."

On their last day, we stood on the side of the road next to their suitcases, waiting for the shuttle to Portland. Mum squeezed me so tightly I could barely breathe. I went to hug my father, but he stiffened and pulled away. I moved toward him to try again, and he turned aside so I couldn't reach him. *Right, that's it*, I thought to myself. *This is how it ends.*

I walked back into the office building opposite the shuttle stop, back to my desk not far from the open window. As I opened the plumbing order forms, I heard a wild and primal sound. It got louder and louder. I ran to the window to see if an injured coyote had appeared on the street. My parents were still standing there. My father was bent over, wailing.

That sound seared through me, through the thoughts, the belief systems, the alienation. It sliced through everything. Despite all that he'd said, and much that he'd done, as the howl pierced the distance between us and lanced my heart, it was entirely clear to me, for the first time since childhood, that my father loved me. A moment later, the road was empty.

THE IDEA OF A PLUM

JUDY REEVES

"I would have never thought of a plum," I say to Tom one July morning, our first summer in the country. We've come down to the orchard, as we often do on these bright mornings. I pluck a plum from a branch near where we stand—it comes off easily—and hold it in my hand, palm open, staring into its deep-purple skin as though some creation story might be imprinted there. "Really, Tom," I say, "how do these things happen?"

"You're supposed to eat the fruit, kiddo, not contemplate it." Tom has his own set of beliefs that don't include such questioning—he plants things, he fishes; he whistles. He sets off down the hill to tend his new avocado trees, hoe on his shoulder, whistling. In his red shirt, this tall, lean Canadian I've fallen in love with reminds me of a rare exotic bird, landed here on his migration to somewhere else. I stand beside the tree with my plum and my questions.

The orchard is planted in tiers, peaches and nectarines above plums and apricots. Further down, the citrus: oranges, lemons, grapefruit; a tangerine at the far end above the slope where the new avocado trees grow. The stone fruit and citrus have been here for some time, farmed and nurtured by the previous owners of this property—a house and acre of land in San Diego's backcountry, a place I never thought I'd find myself after decades of living near the ocean. I, too, feel like a transplant. But Tom loves the land, and I love Tom, and love has its own way of sowing seeds.

Summers get very hot here in the backcountry, and dry. The orchard stays cool with the fruit trees' abundant green leafiness, and the air carries a hint of moisture. I've brought my journal with me and find a shady place under the plum tree to sit and write. The scent of ripe fruit is fairly intoxicating. The ground is still slightly damp from the morning dew, but not too wet, and I sit, lean back against the tree's sturdy trunk, set down my journal and my ripe plum, and take off my sandals. The ground is cool against my bare skin and gives off an earthy, loamy odor that reminds me of long-ago days in the garden with my father. Him explaining how the seeds we drop into the furrows we've made will grow into cucumbers, lettuce, beans on vines so long and leggy, we'll have to stake them up.

"But how?" I ask, looking at the scattering of pale seeds in my hand. "How will that happen?"

"Pay attention," he says. "Be still and watch."

On the hill above me, bees buzz drunkenly among the ripe peaches; the air is rich with a slightly fermented scent. Birds whose names I've yet to learn sing their morning songs, shadow light dapples the full leafing trees. I sit and breathe it all in, not yet opening my journal to write; I will, but for now, I want to be still and listen to the birdsong, the bees, the distant *hack hack*ing of Tom at work with his hoe. I pick up my plum again and hold it in my hand, fingers curled to make a kind of bowl. The plum is slightly overripe and soft, its skin a little puckered where stem held fruit to branch. The deep-purple skin gives slightly, and a tiny rivulet of golden juice leaks onto my palm.

Surrounded by all that lusty life, palm open, holding that overripe fruit, my hand sticky with its juice, I breathe in one fragrant breath after another, and something opens to me. Or maybe *in* me. It is as if I have entered another realm. A sudden brilliance strikes me and all around me shimmers—the branches of trees, their dense leaves and plump, ripe fruit—each detail of the orchard traced in a glittering light. Across the canyon, hillsides glow as if outlined by a golden aura. There are no shadows, only light, which has become a physical presence I can touch, a feeling of not just sun upon my skin, but as if light itself is embracing me, holding me in a longed-for reunion.

For a moment that could have been no more than a nanosecond, a heartbeat, barely a breath, I *understand*. A knowledge comes upon me that is vast and deep and overwhelming. For just that moment, that nanosecond, that heartbeat, I understand the perfect completeness of the rhythms of nature: How the earth holds the roots of the trees, how the sun, the rain, the tule fog that runs through the canyons, the birds, those drunken bees—even me, misplaced and separate as I have been—how all this is vital to the wholeness of the whole. I am as much a part of that plum as the plum to the tree as the tree to the earth as the earth to the sky, to All that is.

I am struck dizzy with this knowledge and lean against the tree to steady myself. Then, just as suddenly as it opened, the door to that clarity, that absolute understanding, closes.

Slowly I become conscious of my physical state—the sure solidity of the tree trunk, its smooth bark against my skin, the damp earth against my bare feet. As the dizziness fades, so does the knowledge, the understanding, the certainty I experienced just the moment before, and the common world I occupy—the orchard, the bees, the morning sun, the damp earth, my closed journal beside me—all is present again. The dappled shadow light of sun, still warm on my skin, is, once again, just sun.

But here, in my hand, I hold the key to that understanding. I know without a doubt that inside the small seed in the center of the ripe plum I hold in the palm of my hand lives the perfect and complete idea of a tree. I hold, as the poet said, infinity in the palm of my hand.

The knowledge, the certainty, the understanding that came to me, completely unexpected and without warning, cannot be explained away in a language I know. It is as my father said all those years ago, "Be still. Just watch." He, too, understanding that words like *photosynthesis, pollination, germination*, and others even more exotic, give names to the process but don't explain the miracle of it. Even as I use the word "miracle," I am merely giving another label to something that can't be reasoned.

All those years living at the beach, I'd been in jaw-dropping awe of the immensity of the sea, but when I thought of myself in relation to its vastness, I saw myself separate and inconsequential. This morning, among the trees in my orchard, I feel connected to something alive and holy, and I know that I am part of some kind of higher order. Something that can't be explained at all. But accepted. Believed. Trusted.

Not too long after that morning, my time in the backcountry came to an end. I'm a city dweller now, and my fruit usually comes from the supermarket or a farmer's market set up in blocked-off city streets. Still, each time I bite into a peach or a plum and let the sweet juice mess my face and sticky my hands, I breathe in the rich, sweet scent of ripe fruit and remember that July morning in my orchard. I don't ask the question "how?" but murmur words that could be a prayer. "Thank you," I say, "thank you."

KILLER BEES

DIANE L. SCHNEIDER, M.D.

Atlanta, Georgia, mid-July 1984

I pulled into the Grady Hospital parking garage at 4:30 a.m. *(Yeah, a.m.)* I hoped that my early start would allow me enough time to see all of my twenty-nine patients before morning report at seven. I put on my white jacket that identified me as a medical intern. When I crossed the street, I took out my pager, turned it on, and clipped it to the belt cinched tight on my white pants. Inside the hospital, I waited for the excruciatingly slow elevator instead of a hike up many flights of stairs.

I had stepped into the empty elevator when a *beep-beep-beep* echoed off the walls. My pager broadcasted, "Call 7B nurses 4731-4731, STAT!"

Oh no, not 7B. I hated to have patients on that floor. They were the notorious Killer Bees. So many bad things happened on 7B, it became known as the Death Star.

I quickly mashed the seventh-floor button. As soon as the elevator stopped, I rushed off, ran down the hall, and breathlessly announced myself at the nurses' station. "Who paged Dr. Schneider STAT?"

A bespectacled nurse with salt-and-pepper hair looked up from the seat where she worked on a chart. "I did," she said brusquely. She rose slowly, straightened her crumpled white uniform, and moved stiffly to the front of the desk. She leaned in close to me and, in a low, hushed voice said, "Georgia Perryman is your patient, right?"

"Yes," I said.

"She passed."

"WHAT!" I blurted out and shook my head in disbelief. "You're saying Miss Perryman is *dead*?"

"Yup, we just found her dead on morning rounds."

"What happened?"

"Dunno."

I pulled out my brown cards that summarized each of my patients from my breast coat pocket and fumbled through the stack, looking for hers. Georgia Perryman, twenty-nine, admitted the night before last with acute pancreatitis from drinking. A serious diagnosis, but in a young person, well, you just didn't expect them to die.

Jesus Christ! How could this happen?

"You got to pronounce her," the nurse announced in a louder voice.

"WHAT?"

"You need to officially pronounce her *dead*," she bellowed. "Here's her chart."

I took the chart from her outstretched hand and walked down the hall to Georgia's room in shock. The patient—MY PATIENT—died. Damn! The notorious 7B nurses lived up to their Killer Bees nickname. I was so mad I could barely see straight.

I paused at the doorway of Georgia's room and took a couple of deep breaths before entering. The glow of the light from above the headboard illuminated her bed. Only her dark hair poked out from under the white sheets. I approached the right side of the bed and pulled back the sheets to her chest. I listened over her heart and heard nothing. I pulled up her eyelids and shone my penlight into her vacant, unresponsive brown eyes. I reached for her right arm. It was cold and . . . already rigid.

Oh my God!

Rigor mortis had already set in. She had to have been dead for hours for that to become obvious. I quickly yanked back the covers all the way to the bottom of the bed so I could look at the rest of her body. Her left arm appeared *enormous*, about three times the size of her right, and it felt like a water-filled balloon.

Jesus, her fluids ended up in her arm instead of her vein. She needed fluid support and didn't get it. How did this happen?

I stormed back to the nurses' station; I wanted answers. But before I could ask my questions, the dictatorial nurse declared, "You need to call the family and let them know she's taken a turn for the worst."

"Turn for the worst?"

"Yup."

"But she's DEAD; the worst has ALREADY happened."

"Well, you can't say that over the phone."

"Why? Why can't I tell the truth?"

"You have to tell them in person, that's the hospital policy."

About an hour later, a page announced that the family had arrived and were waiting in the 7B conference room. I stopped at the 7B nurses' station. "Is the chaplain here yet?"

"No," the clerk at the desk responded.

I dreaded the task before me. This would be my first time delivering the news of a death to loved ones by myself. I expected to find a roomful of relatives wailing loudly. I thought they would ask a barrage of questions and I felt nervous about how to answer them. How am I going to handle this? I felt anything but confident. I briefly steeled myself and headed for the conference room.

Anxiously, I peeked in the window of the door before I pulled it open. Five people, three women and two men, sat around the table. My mouth went dry—how would I get the difficult words out? As I made my way to the table, I recognized Miss Perryman's mother from admission. My heart beat faster. My throat tightened. The conversation ceased. All five sets of eyes followed me in. Everyone was dressed in their Sunday best, the women in floral summer dresses and the men in dark suits. They wore stoic expressions. I expected they knew "Taken a turn for the worst" was Gradyspeak for DEATH. They braced themselves for the confirmation.

I sat down opposite Georgia's mother, who sat stiffly with her hands tightly clasped together in front of her on the table. After we exchanged greetings, she introduced me to her two sisters and their husbands. I nodded acknowledgment and turned back to look directly at Georgia's mother. "Mrs. Perryman, thank you for coming so early this morning. I am sorry to tell you—your daughter passed away during the night."

She appeared calm, quiet. She sat back in her chair and released her clasped hands. Everyone else sat still with their heads bowed as if in prayer.

Would they start questions now? In the silence, I readied myself for the onslaught.

Suddenly, Mrs. Perryman raised her hands high in the air. But she didn't yell, or rant, or question. No, she began to sing in a loud melodious voice, "Swing low, sweet chariot."

I watched in astonishment as everyone joined in; their hands reached up toward the ceiling and swayed side to side.

"Comin' for to carry me home,
Swing low, sweet chariot,
Comin' for to carry me home.

"If you get there before I do,
Comin' for to carry me home,
Tell all my friends I'm comin' too,
Comin' for to carry me home."

I marveled at this unexpected scene; a tear dribbled down my right cheek. I quickly brushed it away and hoped no one noticed.

"That . . . that was beautiful," I said, and took a deep breath. I hated to break the mood in the room after the song, but I wanted to get to the bottom of what caused her daughter's death. "Mrs. Perryman, we don't know exactly what happened. We would like to do an autopsy, so we can find out and learn from it."

Mrs. Perryman placed her hands flat on the table and steadied herself. "Cut her up?" She paused. "Nah. I don't think so."

"It's up to you. We will follow your wishes, whatever you decide, but we'd like to find out why it happened."

"I know what killed 'er."

"Well, I don't think we—"

She interrupted. "She's dun bin pulled green."

"What?"

"Dun bin pulled green before her time. She hadn't any sense. She made bad choices and that dun killed 'er."

"I know this is a shock. But to find the reason for her death, an autopsy would be really helpful."

"Nah, this ain't a shock. I knew she was goin' to an early grave. I've bin prayin'. Maybe that's what got her this far."

A rap on the window of the door interrupted us. The hospital chaplain had arrived. I felt relieved. I had run out of things to say.

"I'm turning you over to the chaplain. Please contact me if you change your mind about the autopsy or if there is anything you need," I said, as I rose to excuse myself.

"You did all you could. Thank you, Doctor," echoed behind me as I left.

I wanted to turn and say, "that's not true." But I tentatively walked into the hallway, stopped, and leaned against the wall for support. I was crestfallen. She was practically my age. I couldn't imagine my life ending now. Her mother's reaction surprised me. She appeared at peace with her daughter's death. No questioning—they even thanked me, for goodness' sake.

Did I—we—do everything we could? NO! The system failed. Was she killed by the incompetence of the 7B nurses or by the actual disease?

We would never know without an autopsy.

Her death hit close to home. One's life was fragile.

She could be me . . . or anyone.

A PERIOD PIECE

TINA MARTIN

Laura was twelve when she got her first period; she had no idea what to expect when her first "monthly bill" came due. "I thought I had raspberry diarrhea," she said, when her dad called me and handed her the phone. Who could blame her? She had no mom to speak of. No one but her dad to explain things he had not experienced. He might have skipped over the menstruation page in the puberty book, or touched lightly on it and jumped straight to the more-relatable changes of acne, body hair, and malodorous feet and armpits.

I hadn't prepared for this call. The period talk was not a conversation I expected to have with Laura when I'd donated the egg that created her to my sister thirteen years earlier. I thought I'd garner favorite-aunt status with Laura if I did things like send timely and hip birthday gifts and check in regularly, even though neither hip gifts nor keeping in touch were my strong suit. What I did expect was an awkward conversation when Laura turned eighteen, when I would sit down with her and my sister and brother-in-law to explain how fertility can be fickle and is often not bestowed upon the most deserving among us and thus, I was genetically her mother, but my sister would always and forever be her mom.

Or maybe not. Because another thing that is fickle? Mental health. And while my sister was the epitome of smart, funny, beautiful, and amazing, with lovely friends, a great husband, and a deep desire, for as long as I'd known her, to be a mom, she had also always struggled with depression. I wanted to believe motherhood would bring out the strongest and healthiest in her, but when Laura was born, my sister's mental health quickly deteriorated. At some point, the fragile dam of her sanity gave way. Then she found solace in alcohol and opioids.

I didn't know how serious the situation was as it was happening. I had moved overseas right after the egg donation, before Laura was even born, and only caught long-distance glimpses of the dire state of things—enough to be worried but hope I was overreacting. I thought I might have been more sensitive to the reports of my sister's behavior, given that I was the genetic mother of the child she was raising. But in truth, I'd never felt like Laura was mine. I'd signed away my rights to her before she was born; I'd been happy to do so. I'd gifted an egg to my sister and relinquished authority over whoever it created. Over Laura. I'd also told myself this relinquishment included the license to judge, blame, and offer unsolicited advice, to feel like "That's not how I would like it to be done" or "I would prefer for you to treat my egg like this." The legal paperwork helped me draw an important psychological line. Laura was no more my daughter than my brother's sons were mine. And if, when I laid eyes on her for the first time, my breath quickened in maternal yearning, well, too bad.

Maybe because I had prepared myself, I didn't feel that yearning. She was two months old when I saw her for the first time on a quick visit home. I wanted to hold her and love and celebrate her, but also, I wanted to inspect her. Does she have my eyes? Is she serious and shy, like I was as a baby? Does she suck the same fingers I did? Does she bear any similarities to my daughter, Sarah, her genetic half-sister? The answer was no to almost everything; she was the spitting image of her dad. I was glad for this. It made the line between mother and aunt even easier to draw.

While I was overseas, my sister's situation continued to worsen. My brother-in-law, after many attempts to ameliorate the crisis, finally divorced my sister when Laura was six. After numerous incidents involving the police and CPS and full psychiatric evaluations for both my sister and brother-in-law, he was awarded full custody.

The police department in Marin had become quite familiar with my sister; she was a "5150"—a danger to herself and others. We knew what she was up to by following her public record; she was regularly arrested and in and out of incarceration.

She was allowed to have professionally supervised custody visits of her daughter once a week, at a list of places with names like "Appleworks," where their visits were overseen by a guard. This was the only way the court allowed my sister to see her daughter, for fear of Laura's safety. The visits proved unsuccessful. My sister was soon banned from the entire list of acceptable supervision facilities for her belligerent behavior. She was paranoid and filled with rage. Soon she had almost no contact with Laura.

I may not have considered Laura my daughter, but I blamed myself for her situation. Why hadn't I known how fragile my sister was? How could I have supported her more, helped her address her issues, relieved some of her burden? Would her problems have mounted to this extreme if I hadn't moved overseas? Or if I'd moved closer than a two-hour flight away when I eventually came home? Was it a mistake to have provided an opportunity at motherhood to someone nature had refused—someone who had proven to be the furthest thing from the optimal recipient? Was I wrong to have entrusted my sister with my egg? How could I fix things now?

I had no answers and, even if I did, no authority. Without my consent, my brother-in-law told Laura I was her biological mother when she was eleven; he did so to ease her mind. She'd been worried that my sister's mental health would pass down to her. I understood his decision, but I also wondered if Laura felt abandoned twice, first by my sister and then by me, her aunt-mother, who invited her to visit for a week at the beach every summer, but otherwise was not a strong, regular influence in her life. I felt tremendous guilt for my part in creating a motherless child.

When I got the menstruation telephone call, my oldest daughter Sarah and I were in Northern California, close to where Laura lived, for a field hockey tournament. "Can you meet us for lunch?" I asked. "We can talk about it."

Laura and her dad came for lunch. We walked to the closest taco shop, ordered at the counter, and sat down. I took the plastic number and wedged it into the sticky metal stand. The four of us—Sarah, Laura, her dad, and I—shared a moment of awkward silence. The sister-cousins stared at their orange sodas. Finally, the words burst forth.

"There are a few important things about womanhood you probably won't read in a puberty book," I started, and then cleared my throat. My brother-in-law's eyes widened but, like a champ, he didn't run. I glanced at Sarah; she responded with the slow, knowing nod of a wily two-year period veteran.

We talked about it for over an hour. Sarah and I took turns telling our worst period stories—the ruined white shorts, the friend's destroyed bed sheets, not wanting to stand up from a chair for fear of the crime scene that might be there. Borrowing sanitary products from a stranger, cleaning jeans in a restaurant bathroom sink, wadding half a roll of toilet paper in underwear. The vacation period, the airplane period, the boat period. The wings, the bleach sticks, the Advil. Tears, cramps, and pimples. If it had happened in the history of womanhood, we went over it.

As luck would have it, there was a CVS right next door. Post-chat, we headed straight to the women's aisle for a tour. "Someday, maybe sooner than later, you'll be so grateful someone invented these." I pointed to the tampons. "Call me when you get to that day. It's not something you'll want to learn via YouTube. For now, stick with these." I pointed to the "sporty" blue and "comforting" green square pillow-shaped bags. "Try a few different kinds to see which are most comfortable for you. Put one in every purse, sports bag, and backpack, plus several in your dad's car with an extra pair of undies. And remember, when in doubt, *wear black.*"

It was unplanned, and yet it was by far the best puberty talk I'd ever been a part of. My talk with Sarah three years earlier had been nowhere near as clear or as comfortable. My mother's talk with me many years before had been a combination of quick, confusing, and mortifying. Laura, in contrast, looked relieved, and happy for the openness. She laughed and asked a lot of questions. My brother-in-law looked shocked and horrified, but mostly, enlightened.

"Please call me anytime you want to talk, or if you have any questions. Nothing is too small or too big. I'm here if you need me," I said. She nodded, looking grateful and smiling at me longer than she ever had, and for the first time I thought, maybe I'm not terrible at this role I've struggled to define. Menstruation might be a topic that is easier to learn about from an aunt-mom than a mom-mom. And then I realized, there could be more topics ahead that will be easier to discuss with an aunt-mom like me. And if that's the case, then perhaps, like Laura, I do belong here, in this awkward and often confounding space. Maybe my role is simply to love her and, when possible, bring levity and clarity to situations that are often anything but light and easy to understand.

My daughter-niece is a gift to me and to this world, and I am beginning to see that I am a gift to her, too. And maybe, just maybe, she has my chin.

WE HAD THE DOG TAGS ALL ALONG

SANDI NIETO

For thirty-five years, this question haunted me: *Where in the world is my father?*

Here's what I knew: My father's name was Leo Thomas Bowden. He was a World War II veteran. He had worked at the US Grant Hotel in downtown San Diego as a chef. He was an alcoholic. We lived as a family in a tiny house in Linda Vista. I had two older sisters. We were a regular family.

Then, one sunny July day in 1954, when I was just two and a half years old, he just up and left. With no warning or explanation, he disappeared from our lives. One morning he was drinking coffee at the kitchen table, and the next day, he was gone—a ghost.

I clung to one wisp of a memory.

I was a toddler playing outside our tiny house. I twirled around the poles that held up our front porch. Mommy was inside cooking a big Sunday dinner. The smells of lemon chicken and cinnamon apple pie wafted on the breeze. The clouds hung low in the sky, and my daddy sat in a chair on the porch, smoking a cigarette.

"Don't do that, you'll fall."

I don't know whether it was said with love or annoyance. It was the only real memory I had.

The only other story about my relationship with him came from my sister Linda. "Daddy would take care of you in the evenings to give

Mommy a break. She'd be hurrying around the house, and he would balance you on his lap, reading the evening news."

That was it. One fuzzy memory on a porch and family lore that once he cared enough to hold me. With the absence of answers, I tried to fill in the blanks. I couldn't put a name to the feeling, but somehow, I knew I was responsible for his disappearance. He left soon after I was born. He already had two daughters, so why would he want me, another girl? It was my fault I was not born a boy.

On some days, I became obsessed with finding answers about what happened to him.

Maybe he got so drunk that he fell on the street, got amnesia, and didn't know who he was. Maybe he was kidnapped. Maybe he owed bad men money or was in jail in Tijuana.

Then other days, like the day he wasn't there to take me to the father–daughter dance, I found myself living in a magical world where I could see the whole movie play out—he would ride up on his white horse and rescue us, rescue me.

The not knowing *why* he left or *where* he was formed a crater-like void. I wasn't sure what hurt worse: missing a father I never knew, or carrying the shame of having a father that would just up and disappear on you.

"What does your dad do?"

"Where's your dad?"

"Why is your dad never in church?"

I learned it was easier just to say, "He's dead."

Mom wore a similar cloak of fear and shame. She carried her secrets alone until one day, when I was in high school, and she took out the two brown boxes that held my father's documents and photos from the war. As we looked over my father's memories, mother confessed: "Honey, I'm so sorry, but the truth is I was never 'married' to your father, Leo. You and your sisters were born out of wedlock."

My heart skipped a beat. It was another piece of the puzzle of my life, and yet, it didn't provide any answers into why Dad left—*or where he was.*

As the years passed, I learned to put on a mask of the entertaining, always-happy mascot. If anyone looked deeper, they would have seen a hollow shell of a young woman.

Until a few sprinkles of unexpected miracles entered my life. I fell in love with Manuel, a handsome Colombian man, my co-worker at the Town and Country Hotel. Reserved but hilarious. Faithful. A year later, we were married. After seven years of traveling and adventures, we started our family—each a gift that brought true joy. I could say I felt . . . almost whole.

***

When I was thirty-six, my mother died, and I became the keeper of my father's two brown boxes. Once again, I glanced over the medals of service, dog tags, and military ID numbers. Then I tucked that box away in a closet. Until . . .

The summer of 1988, six months after my mother's death. All was well in my world, but the questions still haunted me. *Maybe I'm not an orphan. What if I found him now? What if he could meet his grandchildren? Maybe if he saw us, the love would come rushing back.*

I had to take the chance. So early one morning, I called the VA with my father's ID number.

"Ma'am, I see three aliases with that ID number."

What? Dad went by three names?

"Yes, I have the name you provided as your father, Leo Thomas Bowden. But he also went by two other names."

"What does that mean?"

It was then the officer on the phone gave me the news that I had been waiting for all my life.

"Well, ma'am, our records do show his date of death as July 27, 1962, in Cook County, Illinois."

My body froze, my mind went numb.

Date of death? July of 1962? Date of death. He was gone.

"You know, if you can request his death certificate from the county, we can send you all his records. Good luck."

As soon as I hung up, I burst into tears. *He died when I was ten?* All that wasted time dreaming of his return, when he'd been dead for most of my life. It was the end of all my magical thinking. But not the end of the curiosity.

As I cooked dinner, I thought, *What about those aliases?* As I brought my daughter to dance class, I mused, *Who was he, if he wasn't Leo Bowden?*

When I received all of my father's records from the government, I found a treasure trove of clues and a map that led to even more mysteries.

First, there was his rap sheet from the FBI with his drunk and disorderly conduct on three different dates.

Second, there was a letter from an attorney that represented his two sons in search of military insurance. Sons? He had two sons. Were they born before or after my sisters and me? My head was spinning.

Third, there was a letter from a former wife. Was that why he didn't marry my mom? Each document led me further down a rabbit hole. I became driven, almost as if addicted to a drug, to discover more. At times I was half in my present life, half mired in the unanswered questions of the past.

I researched all I could about my half brothers. Before I knew it, I was on the phone with a Mrs. George Mennig, an aunt by marriage.

"Mrs. Mennig, you don't know me, but my name is Sandi Nieto, maiden name Bowden." She seemed nice, open to talking. I continued.

"I think your husband was my father's brother, who left our family in San Diego in the summer of 1954."

"Yes, I think you're right," she said.

The tone in her voice was warm. A small-town woman who was opening her arms and all of her stories to me.

"Your father was the prodigal son that returned to his parents in July of 1954," she said.

"Wait, Leo told my mom that he was an orphan."

"No, I have a photo of your grandparents' fiftieth wedding anniversary with Leonard and his third wife."

"He had three wives?"

The story unfolded. "Leo married his first wife, Dolores, when he was very young. They were married in the Catholic church and had three boys." *I had more half brothers?*

"He wanted to get away from her, but divorce was out of the question. So, on the evening of December 5, 1939, Leo and Dolores went out to dinner with another couple.

"During dinner, Leonard excused himself, possibly to use the restroom, and never returned. He had called for a taxi and drove to the South Shore. He got out of the cab, walked to the water, where he apparently tossed his hat and identification into the lake to make it look like a drowning or suicide, then got back into the taxi and left for good."

Before he even met my mother or me, my father had staged his own death.
Of all his mysteries, that was the one I didn't see coming.

It explained so much, why he didn't marry my mother. Why he could just leave our family without a word—he'd done it before.

I hung up the phone. *My father was the kind of man who would fake his own death to escape his first family.*

Three years later, I watched my oldest daughter attend the school father–daughter dance with my husband. And later that night, as I did our nightly dancing routine, I felt a shift happening within. I put on a Barbra Streisand album and held my kids: dancing with them, rocking them to sleep. In the magic of that night, it was clear; there was no savior on a white horse coming. There was no document or phone call that would make it all make sense or make my father a good man. The hole in my heart would have to be filled by me. As my children fell into a blissful sleep, I sighed. For the first time, I felt the weight of the past lifting off of my heart like a cloud—and I knew two things my father would never know:

The joy of a family I would treasure forever.

The joy of knowing myself, the wise woman I was becoming.

HATCHING

CINDY JENSON-ELLIOTT

Franny is the only person I have ever seen hatch from an egg. Of course, I didn't know she was a person at the time. I thought she was a chicken. I thought she was a classroom science experiment. I thought she was a chance to prove I was a cool, smart teacher.

I was mistaken on all counts.

Franny came from one of six brown eggs I purchased over the internet to hatch in my classroom. I was in my second year of teaching science at a small, independent school. In my thirties, I had gone back to college and taken every science class I could fit into my schedule. I knew a little bit about a lot of things, but not much about anything in particular.

But when my husband lost his job in the recession and I needed work, I saw the position advertised and, much to my surprise, was hired to teach nearly every area of science to nearly every age of child, grades 1–8. My biggest worry was that the parents, many of whom were scientists and engineers, would realize how little I knew, and that the kids would realize I was old and uncool. I wanted my classroom to be a world of "Wow!" I knew classroom pets were a path to awesomeness.

I had always liked animals—in other people's classrooms. My own memories of classroom pets were sensory: the odors of guinea pig urine and aquarium algae. At home, my family had experimented with pet ownership with unfortunate results. Our first pet, a bullfrog named Umbridge, flung herself into the air like a suicidal parachutist and died mid-leap. A lost snake followed. Then an egg case full of praying mantises, a hundred gladiators who lost their heads. Perhaps we weren't meant to be pet owners. Perhaps keeping my own kids alive was enough.

But an incubator in my classroom cupboard caught my eye. What could be cooler than watching eggs hatch? Impulsively, I ordered a half dozen—three Rhode Island Reds and three buff Orpingtons.

When they arrived, I followed rumpled instructions, waited for the incubator to heat up, and gently placed the eggs in their cradles. Then I left them on their own for the night, hoping I would be a good enough hen to hatch out chicks.

For the duration of the incubation, I turned the eggs faithfully, running into my classroom on weekends to rotate their position every few hours. I was terrified I would miss a turn or overheat or under incubate them. I wanted whoever was inside the eggs to survive. I was filled with a deep longing to know that Life—with a capital L—worked as it was supposed to, and a dread that I was a weak link in the great chain of being. I didn't want my own ineptitude to be the cause of someone else's suffering.

At last, hatching day drew near. My students and I spoke to the eggs in the words of Yoda, "Do or do not; there is no try," wished them well, and left them alone for the night.

When I arrived at school the next the morning, I examined the eggs, one by one. Most were smooth and untouched. One, however, had a mark the size of a pinhead on its side.

Over the course of the day, as groups of students trooped in and out, we watched as the tiny pip turned into a triangle, a pointed yellow beak pushing through a leathery membrane, knocking off tiny pieces of shell. By 10:00 a.m., we could see a patch of wrinkled skin. For long periods, the bird was still. Was it resting? Could it die trying to get out? Then, just when we thought all hope was lost—Poke! Tap! The beak would push out another shard. Now we could see damp feathers the color of pale urine stuck to a tiny bald head like a bad comb-over.

My mothering instinct pushed me to help, but the directions on the incubator said not to interfere with hatching; that if you help the chick, it will not be strong enough to survive. But hatching seemed like an impossible task, like the cruelest escape room of all time, trying to flee a chamber the size of your body using only a beak. I felt guilty. I thought this was a science experiment. Instead, it felt like the worst kind of parenting dilemma. If I helped, I would weaken the chick and it would die later. If I didn't help, it could get stuck and die now. My hand shaking, I peeled back the membrane a tiny bit and hoped for the best.

By the end of the day, the chick still had not broken out of her egg and it was time to pick up my kids. I hauled the entire incubator, eggs and all, to my car and took it home, then lifted out the egg and put it on a clean towel in an aquarium with a heat lamp. All evening, from dinnertime to dishes, the chick was hard at work. By bath time, her head was fully visible, and I knew her name: Franny.

My family and I sat vigil as Franny lifted the weight of the world onto her skinny little shoulders and toiled away. By bedtime, she lay flopped on a broken eggshell, legs tangled, stumpy wings askew. We held our breath as she staggered to her pink feet—and fell over, hoisting herself up and falling again and again, until finally, she rose up on wide-spread toes, a proud member of the upright bird brigade. She was the champion, my friends. A rock star chicken. A hero who had just done the hardest thing I had ever seen anyone do: hatch.

Over the next few days, Franny's feathers dried out, filled in, and grew fluffy. Most days, I let her stay home in peace. In the evenings, my children would take her out and let her explore the kitchen table. While my husband read the newspaper, Franny would sit on his knee, poking at the paper with an intelligent tap. She had opinions, Franny did, like any of us.

Other days, I brought Franny back into school for lessons, letting her strut around on the floor inside a circle of knees, as students drew and wrote about her body and behavior. I tried to make the lessons about science, but really, they were about love. Franny was more than a science experiment. She was a beloved member of every class, an Ambassador of Birds.

Despite her intelligence, I realized that perhaps being the lone bird in a class of humans was not the best thing for a social being like a chicken. She needed a posse. A friend brought over chicks, and soon we had a quartet living in a box in the living room. Franny now had her girl group, but she was WITH them, and not OF them. Franny was not a chicken. She was a person. She looked at the others—peeping and fussing—as if they were aliens. She was Einstein in elementary school, and nothing we did could help her bridge the gap between her and her peers. She had just grown up too differently.

When the chicks became pullets—teenagers—it became clear they were getting on each other's nerves. They needed a coop. We built one in the backyard and moved the ladies into their new home.

Chickens were the easiest pets of all. All we had to do was open the coop in the morning, close it at night, and make sure they had food and water. The girls spent the day exploring the yard. When we wanted to give them a treat, we called out "Chick-chick-chick!" and the hens would come running, their fluffy thighs bouncing as they bounded over the grass. Our ladies had a good life! We were, for the first time, successful pet owners. And I was, for the first time, a cool teacher.

Early one morning a few weeks after the school year ended, I went out to open the coop and feed the hens. I could see from the door, though, that the coop was already open. I called out, "Chick-chick-chick!"

No one came running.

I ran around the garden, my steps faltering as I passed a shiny gray rope stretched out on the grass . . .

Intestines.

My heart stopped.

All over the grass, russet down feathers lay like a brown snowfall. In lonely corners, body parts mingled with rusty grass. Mangled tail feathers. A whole, bloodied wing. Entrails, pinkish-brown and slick.

The yard was a crime scene. Whoever had eaten them had run them down, one by one. Chase. Tackle. Death.

It had been so easy to have chickens. Especially a smart chicken like Franny. All we had to do was open the coop in the morning.

And shut it at night. And. Shut. It. At. Night.

NEVER LOOK BACK

NICOLE GIBBS

March 2007, Brunswick, Georgia

What do you take when you are leaving your whole life behind?

I stood at the front door of our townhouse and took a good look around. Stains on the carpet where Taylor, my four-year-old, had spilled her juice. Fingerprints on the walls. Rebecca's framed ten-year-old artwork, two-year-old Jordan's toy trucks lying near the toy box. A box of diapers for five-month-old Emily. *How could I leave it all behind? How could I take any of it?*

I went through a checklist in my mind of all the things we might need. I tried to not think of what I was going to do. I made a last sweep of the house, memories washing over me, smiling slightly at the thought of Rebecca and Taylor flying down the stairs on a tray they had stolen from Mc Donald's.

I didn't cry. I didn't scream and tear my hair out. I didn't have time. If I stopped to feel it, I might get so lost in the pit of despair that was closing in, I would never get out. I would never go. And right now, I needed to go.

I was twenty-seven years old, and overnight I had become a single mom with four kids.

I closed the door behind me, the eviction notice still taped to it. "Eviction due to criminal activity." I pulled the paper down and crumpled it up. I walked a few steps down the path and then turned and flung it at the front door, red-hot rage in the corners of my vision.

The paper hit the door, bounced off, and landed on the welcome mat. I replayed the whirlwind of the past few days in my mind.

It had started with the phone call I received just an hour or so after I had gotten to work two days ago. It was Jeremy.

"I'm at the police station," he had said. "I was arrested."

"Arrested for what?" I had asked, as my stomach clenched and my heart raced.

"I molested Rebecca," he replied.

How had he said those words so easily? How had he just flipped my whole world upside down without even taking a deep breath first?

We had been struggling in our marriage for some time. Jeremy had been using harder and harder drugs. At one point, I had caught him smoking crack. He had wiped out our bank account, spending all of our rent money on drugs. I'd finally had enough just before Emily was born. I had told him that he either had to get clean or leave. He'd started going to Narcotics Anonymous and had gotten a sponsor. He was clean and working the steps. Things had gone from desperate to hopeful.

I don't remember how I got home from work, but there were two police officers waiting for me. There was a worker from the Department of Family and Children's Services there too. They asked if they could come in. They gave me some details. Jeremy had told his sponsor that he had been molesting Rebecca, my now-eleven-year-old daughter, and his sponsor had called the police.

"Do you have any options? Any family you can take the kids to? Anywhere you can go?" the social worker had asked me.

"All of my family is back in California," I told her.

"Honey," she leaned in close and whispered, "if I were you, I would pack up those kids and take them home as quick as you can."

The next day, I had to take Rebecca in for a forensic interview. I had no idea what a forensic interview was, but it sounded scary. We pulled up to a house that had been converted to offices.

"Just tell them the truth," I told Rebecca. She wouldn't look at me.

They took her into one room, and the other kids and I stayed in the waiting room. There were toys for Taylor and Jordan to play with. Emily slept in her car-seat carrier.

"Ma'am, can we have a word with you?" an officer asked me. "Miss Veronica here will stay with the kids while we talk." Miss Veronica was about my age, dressed in a skirt and button-down shirt. I compared it to my own dirty jeans and stained T-shirt. I hadn't slept. Had I even brushed my hair? She was probably more qualified to look after my kids than I was. I followed the officer into a small room with a large table. Another officer sat at the table, a stack of papers in front of him.

"Have a seat," the first officer said. He was younger, with a sharp brown mustache and military style haircut.

I sat down across the table from them. The older officer was not in a uniform. He had lines around his blue eyes and gray hair at his temples that made him look tired.

"So, how much of this did you know?" the younger officer asked.

"What do you mean?" My mind was blank. I didn't understand the question.

"You had to have known something was going on." His eyes bored into my soul.

Did they know about my suspicions? About the time I had confronted Jeremy, only for him to convince me that I was horrible to even think there might be something not quite right about him spending so much time reading her bedtime stories? Could they know about him making me feel like I was insane, like there was something seriously wrong with me to suspect that he had anything other than the best of intentions? He had stepped up to the plate when her biological father had dropped off the face of the earth, after all. He had chosen to be her father.

"Your husband is being charged with ten counts of child molestation," the older officer said gently. "He claims that you had some knowledge of this."

My stomach lurched.

"I think I am going to be sick," I said.

The younger officer began to recount details to me. The room spun. I jumped up and made it to the trashcan by the door just in time.

Why would Jeremy tell them that I knew, when he had made me feel crazy when I had confronted him? How could he have done all of this? What about the life we had planned, our hopes and dreams? How could he betray all of us like this? How could he abuse my daughter? Had he done anything to the other kids?

It was at that moment that I had decided we were leaving Georgia. I had to get home. I had to get back to my family where I was safe, where my kids would be safe.

I had spent the next twelve hours pacing our townhouse, packing, making phone calls, planning. I didn't want to leave my friends, my home, my career. I had built a whole life in Georgia, and as much as I missed my home in California, it hurt my heart to think about leaving everything behind.

I only told a few people I was leaving. My parents, my boss at Applebee's, my friend Felicia. I didn't tell Jeremy's parents. I was tired of asking them for help that they always withheld, and I knew that they would do anything they could to make me stay.

***

The kids were secured in their car seats, all of them except Rebecca, who was sitting in the front passenger's seat, a map of the United States spread out on her lap. As we drove toward the Florida border to get to I-10, I felt my anxiety rising. What if Jeremy's parents called the police? Could they stop me? Would they take my kids? I felt like I was kidnapping my own children. The closer we got to the border, the more anxious I felt. I tried not to let on to the kids. I didn't want them to worry. We sang songs as I gripped the steering wheel, my hands sweating.

Nothing in the van worked. There was no gas gauge, no speedometer, no odometer. I had to determine how much gas we were using by the mile markers. *This is ridiculous. I should go back.*

My mind raced with endless scenarios. Maybe this was just some big mistake. Maybe Jeremy had just lost his mind because of the drugs, maybe he hadn't really . . .

I looked over at Rebecca. At eleven years old, her body was starting to morph into that of a young woman's. Had he really done those things?

I wasn't wrong. I hadn't been wrong. Not at all.

I couldn't go back.

"Rebecca," I said.

"Yes, Momma?"

"Have you thought any more about what we talked about yesterday?"

"Yeah," she said softly.

"Baby, I need to know . . . did he touch you like that?"

"No, Momma." The lie filled up all of the empty space in the car.

USS *VINCENNES*

JAMES ROBERTS

When people talk about the day of a disaster, they often say, "The morning started out under a clear, blue sky"—a tragedy seems more tragic if the weather is nice. But this day started grudgingly, with a smudgy blob of sun trying to penetrate the grit and humidity of the Persian Gulf air. People also tend to say, "The day started off just like any other," so I guess that part held true.

The morning was stifling, just like every day in the Gulf. If there was a difference, it was the blissful ignorance of what was in store for me that day and how it would affect my perspective on American infallibility. I used to have *Titanic* levels of confidence in our military, just like the architect of the "unsinkable" boat now at the bottom of the Northern Atlantic. But today, I would have a front-row seat for a failure that ended up in a two-inch font on the front page of every newspaper in the world.

It was July 3, 1988, and I was a young helicopter pilot deployed on the USS *Vincennes*, a navy cruiser equipped with the state-of-the-art Aegis weapon system. My official mission was to keep a watchful eye on the Iranian navy, which had been harassing commercial shipping coming through the volatile Strait of Hormuz. But my unofficial mission was class clown, providing comic relief for the wardroom during the oppressive grind of this *Groundhog Day* cruise.

Up to that point, our dealings with the Iranians had been predictably boring, and during my flights, I was predictably bored. But intelligence reports indicated a likely attack over the July 4th holiday. That's why our bosses wanted the firepower of the *Vincennes* in the Gulf. So, prepped for this possible threat, our crew began the day with the anxiety of a kindergarten class anticipating their first fire drill.

My helicopter pulled the fire alarm. When we spotted several Iranian patrol boats menacing a Panamanian freighter, we headed that way to provide some adult supervision. On a normal day, that would have been enough to send the Iranians on their way. But the boats unexpectedly fired shots at our aircraft. Outgunned, I flew away, radioing the equivalent of "Mom, they're shooting at us!" The *Vincennes* charged in to engage the patrol boats while, fifty miles away, an Iranian commercial airliner taxied for takeoff.

There's a reason the *Vincennes* was the first Aegis cruiser to ever enter the Strait of Hormuz. Its technology was more suited to open-ocean warfare than to the beehive of the Gulf. The ship wasn't well-suited to attacks from insignificant threats like patrol boats. One critic likened it to an elephant being harassed by a pack of hyenas. It was also a hideous place to fly a helicopter, with conflicting territorial restrictions and perpetually poor visibility. Each day I landed safely was one more I could cross off my calendar until we left this hellhole. My letters home expressed more fear of being shot down by friendly fire than by any enemy.

While the *Vincennes* exchanged gunfire with the Iranian patrol boats, Iran Air flight 655 took off from Bandar Abbas International, a combination civilian–military airport. For reasons that involved both human error and the complexities of an overloaded data network, the information that was passed to the ship's captain made the airliner appear more threatening than it actually was. Instead of climbing, our captain was told the aircraft was descending. Instead of displaying a common identification code for civilian aircraft, he was told the aircraft was showing the code for an Iranian fighter jet. Self-fulfilling expectations and an evangelical belief in the "church of technology" had set the ship up for disaster.

As the drama unfolded, I was excited to watch our training put to use in something other than a simulator or an exercise. This was real combat, and it was exhilarating. I heard the order to "Cover track 4131." I was familiar with the term "cover." It's when fire-control radar is aimed at an aircraft, the preliminary step before actually shooting a missile. Several minutes passed as we became more and more concerned with the perceived attacker. I strained to follow the rapidly deteriorating situation over the radio. The slip of a few expletives by my usually professional crewmates betrayed their anxiety.

When I heard the order, "Take track 4131," I looked over to the pilot next to me and asked, "What does 'take' mean?" I got my answer in the form of a seismic shudder. It looked and felt like the space shuttle was lifting off, as two surface-to-air missiles the size of telephone poles raced toward the unsuspecting airliner. Then, with the final radio call, "Splash track 4131," 290 souls lost their lives.

For a few minutes, I had that surreal out-of-body feeling, as if watching a movie. The adrenaline from a successful enemy engagement rippled through the ship's communication channels. *Had I really just witnessed the downing of an enemy fighter jet?*

The realization that something unthinkable had happened didn't come until later. It was an agonizing faucet drip of comprehension: an airliner was overdue in Dubai, Iranian radio chatter talked of bodies floating in the water. It wasn't until the next day that the captain addressed the crew and confirmed that we had shot down a commercial airliner. It was devastating news. And despite my agnostic faith in God, I still expected a miraculous plot change—some kind of divine mulligan.

The Iranians balked at letting us provide search-and-rescue assistance, which I could understand. We had shot down an airliner like a clay pigeon. *Why would the Iranians think we would be helpful in picking up the pieces?* Besides, there was nothing to rescue. The grisly sight of bloated, naked bodies as I flew over the wreckage confirmed that. My default reaction was to support the actions of my crewmates, but I was incredulous that this state-of-the-art warship could have caused the devastation I was seeing.

The investigation that descended on the *Vincennes* brought about the second-guessing that only a major fuckup can provoke. Armchair admirals dissected the shootdown like a morgue autopsy. As the scrutiny intensified, the atmosphere on the ship was funereal. Where normally there was a fraternity house vibe, it became a banter-free zone.

Passageway conversations were conducted in murmurs, and meals were muted affairs. As a member of the helicopter detachment, I was largely out of the investigation spotlight, so I assumed the role of consoler-in-chief to my embattled friends. While my secondary duties as court jester took a backseat, they didn't disappear entirely, but it was like trying to lift the mood of a grieving family.

It was uncomfortably quiet in the eye of the international shitstorm we had caused. But around me, the winds of condemnation and blame raged, as did Iranian officials with threats of revenge. The navy decided to anchor the ship out at sea for our own protection. Navy dolphins (the marine mammal kind) patrolled underwater, and navy SEALs (the human kind) patrolled the surface.

For the next month, my only escape from the ship was an occasional trip to the military port in Bahrain. Even then, I felt like a high-profile defendant being escorted in and out of a courthouse. Counselors came on board to help the crew deal with the enormity of the incident. I found my emotional reaction to what had happened to be disturbingly indifferent. I felt nothing about the loss of life, which was concerning since I can be brought to tears by Humane Society commercials. I didn't lose one hour of sleep over the deaths of these innocent people. I didn't look away as I had flown over the bodies. I waited to feel some sign of empathy, but it never came. I felt disconnected from every emotion except the guilt of not feeling guilty. I wondered if something inside me had been permanently scarred. I've since learned that my reaction wasn't uncommon—a primitive form of mental self-preservation.

After weeks in public-relations quarantine, I developed the at-sea version of cabin fever. Time dragged as if I were working off a prison sentence. To add to the mood of isolation, I had very little sense of our country's take on the tragedy. In that era before social media, I wondered what the American people were thinking. My anxious mind imagined we might have to enter the witness protection program when we returned home. Older crewmembers remembered the blowback from atrocities in Vietnam and feared a rekindling of public animosity.

But then, the mail started coming in. Not just a few letters. I'm talking *Miracle on 34th Street* bags of mail, almost all professing undying support and appreciation for the crew of the USS *Vincennes*.

A communal sigh of relief went through the ship as we realized we were not going to be treated like lepers on our return. Plus, answering the literal boatload of mail gave everyone something to do.

Coming home, though, I felt like a curfew-breaking teenager, still a bit wary of what kind of reception we would get. I was conflicted, watching the welcome unfold as the *Vincennes* entered San Diego Bay. Tugboats sprayed arcing jets of water, news helicopters circled overhead, and well-wishers lined the shore. Pier side, I walked off the ship's bow to shouts of "Welcome home!" and "God bless America!" I felt like a returning hero, until I remembered I wasn't. Actually, it felt a bit grotesque to be celebrated when the most consequential thing we'd done could be placed in the "debacle" category. But America has become very forgiving of her military, even when sailing home with an epic failure as baggage. President George H.W. Bush even came to our defense with the head-scratching declaration that "I will never apologize for the United States. I don't care what the facts are . . . I'm not an apologize-for-America kind of guy." With supporters like that, who needs a lawyer?

Even sensational news fades after a generation. But I still get asked about that day occasionally. My takeaway?

Just because your morning starts out under a clear, blue sky doesn't mean there's not an iceberg waiting with your name on it.

A WOMAN I NEVER MET

VINCENTIA SCHROETER

I am jarred by the sound of a ringing phone. I open my eyes slightly and look around my bleak hospital room. It has been five days since I lost my second baby. Both were ectopic pregnancies, and just a few short hours ago, I was in danger of bleeding to death. Yesterday, the doctor gave me the news: "You will never be able to have children naturally." I plunged deep and felt like I was under dirt, nearly smothered, unable to breathe.

I hold onto a small light in the dark—Mom is supposed to call, and I feel some hope for connection. She had promised to fly in from San Jose to San Diego and take care of me as soon as I got out of the hospital, which is tomorrow. The phone rings and I hear my mother's voice. My heart jumps in joy.

I expect her to say, "I will be on the next plane." Instead, she says, "I cannot come until later in the week." A familiar fogginess fills my brain as I fold into myself.

It was always like this, growing up in the sixties with twelve brothers and sisters. I would enter the house after walking home from school alone and want to tell Mom

- that I won the spelling bee and earned a plastic statue of the Blessed Virgin Mary,

- that I am mad that Sister Teresa hit my bare legs with a stick,

- that a blond girl laughed, saying that since there were so many of us, each one of us must be "mediocre."

I didn't say any of those things. Mom was busy tending to kids who were yelling louder than I was.

As I look down at myself in the hospital bed, I think of Mom as this post-World War II woman who, after her wedding ceremony in 1945, was asked by her priest, "Ramona, how many children are you going to have?"

With a beaming smile she answered, "Oh, about a dozen." Both my parents wanted a big family, and she ended up birthing those twelve children. She was "Fertile Myrtle." I was the fourth child, and it seemed like I always saw her from behind. At the ironing board. At the stove. At the sink. At the washing machine. Her hands forever busy.

Back in my hospital bed, I shrug. "Okay, Mom. Bye." I hang up the phone, hurt, even though I know this is just a delay. I am as frail as a threadbare blanket. I feel like my umbilical cord has detached from the mother ship and I am floating alone in space. I need something to hold on to. I grab a pillow and press my forehead into it. I gulp back tears, tighten my spine, and take a breath.

When my husband Steve and I leave the hospital the next day, I am forced to go home empty-handed. No baby, no mother. My body has been violated and my heart has been broken. I feel like a failure. We travel forty-five minutes from the hospital to our home in silence. I close my eyes. I don't want to know what is going on outside the car window. Once home, I drag myself out of the passenger-side door in the carport of our humble beige condo. As I walk around the corner to enter our home, I burst out crying. When I left this place, I was pregnant; now I am not and never will be.

I take to my bed and let it swallow me, as I slowly recover from surgery. A few days later, Steve picks up my mother at the airport and I hear their voices as she arrives. My heart pounds with longing, then switches to fear, as I tell myself that Mom will be of little comfort, that she won't understand this pain at all.

Soon I can hear my mother's footsteps coming down the hall. I rub the soft edge of the blanket between my fingers. As she appears in the doorway, I have two strong urges; one is to hide, the other is to be held. My head is spacy, but my body feels tight. I can't move.

Mom enters my bedroom. I can't tell her I am disappointed that she arrived days late.

She walks toward my bed—short, solid, and a little speedy, with a small, sturdy old family suitcase with weathered leather straps that she places on my bed. I look at her for only a second, glancing briefly at her with coldness covering my hurt. She stares at me with compassion, which stings because I cannot take it in.

She is eager to be helpful, and she unlocks and reaches into her suitcase.

"I brought you the doll you had as a child." She pulls out a smiling glamorous woman doll in a strapless black-velvet dress. Is this doll on her way to some party? The 1950s plastic toy has a vapid red-lipstick smile and flirty eyes. I am mute. Mom realizes the doll is not working. She does not give up. Next, she pulls out a brush and comb.

"Would you like me to braid your hair like I did when you were little?"

I am taken aback, surprised she is returning to our childhood routines.

"No," I say. My mind went down a dark road, recalling the morning in third grade when Mom was rushing to braid my long hair, as Dad yelled that we were running late for school. So, my mother grabbed scissors and cut four inches off my braids—without even asking. I shivered a little and frowned as she finished braiding the few inches that were left. She never did apologize, and I never complained. We moved in a pack. It was part of my survival to keep up and keep going. No time for complaints.

I don't need my party-girl doll. I don't want little-girl braids. But I let it in a little that she is trying. She gets it too, that these efforts are not helpful. I look into her eyes with longing. My head feels tense. I'm stuck.

She slowly closes her suitcase, moves to the back of my bed, and looks at me with searching eyes.

"What can I do for you?"

I shrug, "I don't know."

She looks into my eyes and says, "I am so sorry."

I look up into her eyes. "I . . . I lost my baby."

And then she looks at me with compassion and says, "What a terrible loss. I feel so sad for you."

As her words sink in, my body relaxes some, as I feel seen by her.

She had moments like this, where she paused and paid attention to our needs. But they were rare, and we all understood why. She worked thirty-six-hour shifts as a mother and housewife, and any extra need beyond feed, clothe, and bathe, would be met (if at all) by someone running on fumes. I never saw her weak. If she suffered, she never showed it.

This is how I see her, cheerfully pregnant, strong sturdy body doing endless housework and taking efficient care of easily born babies.

Mom looks at me firmly. I hear a sorrow in her voice I have never heard before.

"You know, I had two miscarriages. One after Kenny was born and one after Maria was born."

I am shocked by this information. My eyes grow as big as saucers. She continues, her voice heavy with grief. I am riveted to the spot, because she has never been this vulnerable with me before.

"Their loss hit me hard. I think of those two as souls sitting next to Jesus in heaven. I pray to them every day."

I stare at a woman I have never met.

She lost two babies? They stay in her heart? She thinks of them every day? I am stunned. It feels like my head is exploding and the hard-set pixels are trying to rearrange into something new. They turn into a meadow with sweet yellow flowers. I look at my mother and her face is gentle and soft. She has met me on the field of grief.

I feel held.

Like she saw me coming, turned to face me, and made room on her lap, where I could climb up and lay my weary head against her warm bosom. For as long as I needed. Backed up, mother to daughter. Mother to mother. Mothers who lose babies, mothers who mourn lost babies.

ONE THOUSAND OMS

KIMBERLY JOY

Three months before my thirtieth birthday, when I got diagnosed with lupus, a life-threatening autoimmune disease, I did not pray, because I did not believe in a higher power. I grew up in a house where there was no talk of the spiritual—religious or mystical. The closest thing we had to prayer was when my dad would joke, "God is good. God is great. Yay God. Now let's eat." I developed an unconscious belief that I was "going it alone." Without the idea of someone or something there to catch me when I fell, I made sure I wouldn't fall. I relied on my intelligence and what seemed concrete, infallible: science. I trained in western medicine as a physical therapist, further solidifying my belief that if I couldn't understand things rationally, then they couldn't be real.

I learned lupus causes the body to attack itself, with symptoms that range from mild joint pain to kidney disease to death. Though reeling with shock, I had to choose a treatment plan, and since Western medicine was the only path I knew, it was the obvious choice. My doctor said, "You'll most likely have kidney involvement. We need to start medication right away." Although I worried about the potential side effects of medication, I assumed I could take it and move on with my life.

I couldn't have been more wrong.

We tried drug after drug, each causing side effects that pulverized my system like a wrecking ball: vision problems, night blindness, liver toxicity, pancreatitis. One medication caused such a severe allergic reaction that my eyes swelled shut and my lips looked like two balloons. On another, my long blond hair came out in handfuls. I would stand outside after a shower, run a comb through my hair, then pull wads of hair off the comb and let it go into the wind.

In August of 2003, four years after my diagnosis, a dangerous lupus flare with blood and organ involvement put me in the hospital for the second time within eighteen months. Three weeks into treatment, my doctor sat on the edge of the bed and said, "We've exhausted all of our medication options except Cytoxan, a two-year chemotherapy protocol." My chest constricted. "I know that's not something you want to do. It's your choice, but you need to decide by this afternoon. Either we start chemotherapy tomorrow, or we'll need to do the paper-work to send you to hospice."

I was thirty-three years old.

I remembered being on an African safari years before, watching a cheetah hunt a gazelle. Death was chasing me with the same speed and intensity with which the cheetah had pursued its prey. Like the gazelle, I'd been running at full speed, dodging and weaving to escape. But now it was as if death was in its final leap toward me, midflight, claws outstretched, about to land on my back. I wanted to live, so I reached out a shaky hand and signed my name on the chemotherapy consent form.

The chemo treatments were brutal; my body screamed in dissent after each one. Everything hurt. The sound of a page turning hit my ears as loudly as blasting trumpets—my hands shook and my heart leaped. I slept for only two hours at a time and walked circles around the house at 3:00 a.m., rubbing my chest to ease the nausea and heart-burn, repeating to myself, "just breathe, just breathe."

A year into my chemo-induced zombie-like existence, my doctor called with more bad news: the lupus wasn't responding to treatment. The toxicity from the chemo was sucking the last bits of vital energy from the marrow in my bones. What was supposed to be helping me was killing me.

Western medicine was no longer working.

The enormity of that truth hit like a fist in the gut. My eyes welled with tears as I sat listlessly, staring out the window. My throat tight-ened, strangled by the sobs I held in. I dropped my head into my hands. *I'm out of options.* The cheetah of death that had been pursuing me had finally landed. I was pinned under its weight. I could feel its breath and see its fangs ready to plunge into my neck. One thought kept repeating itself: *I don't want to die.*

From the murky gray depths of my despair, a memory floated to the surface. Months ago, during a massage, the massage therapist had told me that I needed to see Ariel, an energy worker, a woman who could see and feel energy and work with it to help people heal. I'd pretended I was asleep. However, at the end of my massage, the massage therapist handed me Ariel's business card and said, "You should be open and call Ariel for a session." I took the card, but when I got home, I threw it into the bottom of my junk drawer.

Flicks of snow hit the window, drawing me back to the present. I opened the junk drawer and sifted through papers until I found the card. I stared at it as if it could give me the answers I needed. But all it offered was a black background with a single word splashed in bold blue letters, "Ariel," and in smaller print, the words "energy healer" and a phone number. I flipped the card over and over. *She's probably a sham.* I set the card down and pushed it away.

What if she's not? I paused in a moment of uncertainty. I stood at the brink of a precipice, the edge of the known. I imagined that stepping into the dark abyss of the unknown would send me spiraling in an endless fall toward nothingness. If I wanted to survive, I would have to launch myself off the precipice and hope that something, anything, would save me from the fall.

I picked up the card again, thinking, *I'll just call and ask how she works. I won't make an appointment.* I sat frozen in indecision. Finally, I reached for my phone and dialed. My heart pounded in my throat as the phone rang. When Ariel answered, I asked, "What is energy work? What do you do?"

Her voice was soft and melodic. "I allow angels to work through me," she said. "They show me blocked energy, where it is not flowing. I can see torn places in your energy grids, and I use my hands to sew the tears. The angels help me clear energy; then, they send light that pours over you, so you feel peaceful."

I made an appointment. The fearful part of me, the part that found safety in the known, was unconvinced. I didn't believe in energy work, but I was desperate and willing to try anything to stay alive.

During my first session with Ariel, my skepticism kept me tight-lipped. I was purposefully vague about why I was there; I only told her that I had lupus. I expected her hands to move directly over a large scar on my stomach from the surgery I'd had while hospitalized. Instead, she stopped beside my right shoulder, her fingers spinning rapidly above it. "What's wrong with your shoulder?"

"Nothing," I replied.

"Are you sure?"

"Yes."

She continued to question me, certain there was a reason her hand had stopped there. Finally, I remembered my shoulder had a metal pin from a long-ago surgery. "That's what it is," she replied, then her hands moved on. I'd been wearing a T-shirt that covered the scar. How could she have known?

Over time, other experiences continued to put chinks in my armor of resistance and disbelief. During a session when I was too sick from a recent chemo treatment to drive and see her in person, Ariel talked to me on the phone from her office and said, "My hands are working over your stomach to remove nausea. I keep seeing blue-corn chips. They're what's making you feel sick." Chills ran up my body. I'd eaten soup and blue-corn chips for lunch.

I continued my weekly sessions with Ariel. Though I felt relaxed and peaceful after each session, I did not see or feel the energy Ariel talked about. Even with my building trust, I still wasn't convinced the power she worked with even existed, and if it did, I figured you had to have a special gift, like she did, to access it.

About six months later, I was in the middle of a session. Ariel walked, fluid like a butterfly, around and around the table. Her black pants and billowing white top fluttered with her swaying, dancelike movements. Her hands hovered above me, fingers moving rapidly in the air. Unexpectedly, she stopped by my head at my left side and turned her cupped hands up, shoulder-width apart, as if they were holding something substantial. Keeping her hands in that position, she slowly side-stepped toward my feet. It looked as if she was dragging something heavy and dangerous down and off my body. When she reached my feet, she turned with outstretched arms and walked to the corner of the room. Cautiously, she lifted her hands upward, and with a forceful exhale, released what she was holding. She returned to the table and stood motionless by my side.

"I just removed a layer of death from you."

"I'm not surprised," I replied. Inside, my body had felt gray, ashen, like the charred remains of wood after a campfire, about to dissolve into a pile of ash with the slightest breeze, or be blown away in a puff of smoke, into the ethers. "What does death look like?"

"Shh. Be quiet. I need to wait and see what happens. The angels never have me stand still like this." She stood rigid like a stone pillar, arms by her sides. I lay on the table, waiting for what seemed like minutes, but could have been mere seconds.

Suddenly, I felt a rush of something like liquid sunlight, viscous but with some fluidity—like warm honey—flood into the right side of my body. In the same heartbeat, Ariel whispered, "Here they come." The sensation of liquid sunlight continued to flow into me, warming my body to its core, and enveloping me like a golden cocoon. A tingling vibration that pulsed, similar to the inner body vibration created by humming but exponentially more powerful, filled my body. I'd never felt anything like it.

Ariel's hands lifted from her sides and began to work over me again. "The angels are having me weave golden light around you, anchoring it in your center. They are circling around and around you, filling you with light." The vibrating sensation continued to move through me, feeling as if one thousand Oms reverberated in unison within my body. My breath slowed almost to stillness. Tears rolled from my eyes and pooled in my ears.

When Ariel finished, she stood at my feet, lifted her arms over her head, and sealed my energy field. "Rest and let the healing integrate," she said, as she left the room. My body felt heavy, melded to the table. I closed my eyes and became aware of two hazy figures, somewhat resembling human form, muscular and broad-shouldered but more like amorphous bundles of light and energy, standing like sentries at my feet. I felt their presence as much as one can sense a lover across a room. I had never before felt so utterly and completely loved.

My heart cracked open in awe, as I settled into a new knowing, one of the Soul rather than of the mind. I lay in the space of my new known, bathed in a raw and irrefutable truth—the mystery of the unknown was not falling terrified into the nothingness of a black abyss, but instead, floating gently in the arms of angels.

THE SKY IS FALLING

NANCY MAE JOHNSON

In the most traumatic moments of my life, humans have fallen from the sky. I suppose, like some of Chicken Little's friends, you might not believe me. Well, the whole truth is that the first fall wasn't literal. But it was real. It was a scene from my own teenage cautionary tale . . . metaphorical, you might say. It was a fall from my childhood dreams of what could have been, if fairy tales and fables really came true. But in the second and third falls, two men literally fell from the sky to their deaths, leaving me searching for the moral to such tragedy.

My metaphorical fall: I've always loved fairy tales and fables. My father was my first Prince Charming, and I truly believed there was a young man in my future that would fill his shoes. The fables—which often included a trickster and a cautionary lesson—were endearing, but nothing to be concerned about. And so, the story begins.

When I was sixteen, I kissed my first boyfriend in the front seat of his green Mustang Fastback, and I dreamt of what it would be like for him to kiss me at a candle-lit altar. We kissed a lot after that, and when we were eighteen, we married. We got our first cozy apartment, and I kissed him off to work each day. I went to the local community college during the day for a semester. Then I gave up my education to get a stable job, because his jobs never lasted long. Sometimes he stumbled home late at night. My tearful questions evoked righteous anger, and he jabbed his fists into the nearest surface, bloodying his knuckles.

Stuck in my imaginary world, I didn't see the holes in the walls. I didn't hear his screaming voice. I didn't smell the alcohol or the infidelity or the blood from my nose when it hit the steering wheel. I didn't feel anything during the darkest fight, when he sliced his arm open on the wall sconce and had to go to the emergency room to be stitched back together. "God dammit, Nancy! Why do you make me so angry?"

I thought if God or the stork or some power greater than me would part the clouds and let a bundle of love fall through, all the broken places in our fable would be fixed. But after our son was born, our marriage ended anyway. I looked up to the sky falling all around me, and I asked for answers that would ground me. What kind of job will support my son and me? How will I pay my bills, buy groceries, raise this child alone?

My father's fall. Ten years after my teenage fall, my father fell from the sky, too. His fall was even more unexpected than mine. I was twenty-eight by then and had been remarried for four years. My father was fifty-two. He had been my stability when my teen husband was not. When I called my father late at night, sobbing because the baby wouldn't stop crying, he drove right over. He rocked my son through the night, calming his screams through his many ear infections. My father created an unofficial partnership where he owned half the house so he could pay half the house payment. He often whistled up the front walk, arms laden with groceries or tools or hugs. He picked me up and carried me during my own fall.

He was supposed to work part-time in his Lemon Grove shoe store and vacation in Washington at their cabin. He was supposed to grow old loving my mother as they sipped their morning coffee on their deck overlooking the Puget Sound.

Instead, on a sunny, clear February day when he was done with his coffee, my father went out to trim a thirty-foot pine tree. He wanted to top the tree so that he could enjoy a more perfect view of the still, blue waters surrounding Heron Island. My mother said to him that morning, "Leonard, do you have to trim those trees yourself? It's dangerous." The family story is that my father said, "Mary Lou, if I die today, I have done everything in my life that I wanted to do." Less than an hour later, he fell from the sky when the tree top cracked and snapped around, knocking him out of his temporary nest. He was life-flighted to the nearest hospital in Seattle, but my mother knew he was already dead.

A young man's fall. Thirty years after my father fell, I witnessed a young man fall out of the sky to his death.

I was fifty-eight, and like Chicken Little, I had figured out over time that what kept hitting me over the head was not the sky. Generational addiction affected the son of my teenage marriage, but also my second husband. Through recovery, I learned that I had a part in the chaos of my home. I finally turned to therapy to examine my past, learn to take responsibility for my choices, and work on replacing fear, insecurity, and blame with serenity, courage, and personal responsibility.

When I pulled into my therapist's parking lot that fall day about twenty minutes earlier than my appointment, I envisioned some quiet time to journal or listen to the radio. I chose a parking spot facing west, the seventeen-story Marriott Hotel looming in front of me. I relaxed against the driver's seat, feeling warmed by the late-afternoon sun against the black upholstery. From my nearly prone position, I could see the balconies and windows of the high-rise Marriott.

A young man came out onto the balcony one story from the top of the building. Being a writer, I imagined his story: "Where is he from? Why is he staying at the Marriott? Why did he come out on the balcony? What is he drinking? Water? A midafternoon cocktail? What does he have in his right hand? A cigarette? A joint? Did he step out for a smoke break?"

He flicked whatever it was from his hand and let it fall over the rail. He turned quickly and went inside. "Is there drama behind the curtains fluttering in the open doorway? Was he fighting with someone before he stepped out to cool down? Or did his cell phone ring to confirm plans in the Gaslamp District for dinner and clubbing later?"

He was gone for a minute or two, so I focused on my story details. I had time to count over five windows from the left, one floor from the top before he returned to the balcony. He walked without hesitation over to the balcony rail and put both hands on top of the rail. He lifted one leg over the rail, straddling it like a horse. He looked around at the other windows and balconies, and then took a sweeping look below him.

I brought my seat up a notch and my make-believe story faded out as I questioned the more-desperate reality. "What the hell? Hang on, dude. That's not safe."

His right leg followed his left, and he faced the rail so his back was to me. He was now hanging—legs straight down—on the outside of the balcony, both hands gripping the rail. He did a chin-up on the rail. Then, keeping his legs straight and tight together, he brought them from the hanging position up, parallel to the balcony rail, like Superman about to take off in the sky.

I popped my seat fully upright and pressed my face as close to the window as I could. My mother instincts were alert now, and my hand reached for the door handle—but froze there. "Is he exercising on the wrong side of the balcony rail? These are not the Olympic highlights; if he slips, the drop is sixteen stories."

He swung his legs back down to the hanging position with his Superman strength and held onto the balcony rail with his right hand only, doing a one-handed side pull-up. When his body was perfectly aligned, not facing me, legs straight, his left arm at his side, he simply let go and dropped through the air as if he was going to stick a perfect landing coming off the parallel bars.

My heart was pounding, and my hands shook with the possibility of what I had just seen. I dialed 911 and said, "I just watched someone jump off the balcony one floor from the top of the Mission Valley Marriott Hotel."

She said, "I'll send an ambulance."

My voice crumbled and my heart accelerated. I said to the operator, "I think I'm realizing what just happened." My body shook from my lips down to my toes. I ended the call, got out of my car, and walked for a slow-motion eternity across the parking lot to the Marriott.

The young man's body lay directly next to the building, not even one inch from the wall. How had his body stayed so close to the building as it fell sixteen stories? A hotel employee joined me, responding to a call from a resident who had seen a person fall past her window. He shook his head from side to side, and I asked, "Is he gone?" He said, "Yes."

***

The images of those who have fallen from my sky haunt me on some days. On some days, I see the trickster on his path across the sky. On some days, I can sit in awareness of the falls that have taught me that I don't choose who leaves or climbs or jumps. But on most days, I am blessed with the thought that no matter the unstable sky, no matter how many times I fall, something pulls me back up, and I keep walking.

MOM'S NIGHT OUT AND THE TRICKSTER

TANIA PRYPUTNIEWICZ

I'd had a bad year. Like leaving-your-husband-for-ten-days bad. That's what you do when you find photos of another mom-of-three in a negligee while scrolling through family vacation photos over a cup of tea with your daughter. My husband was in a different city earning money from side gigs while I was driving the back roads at home with a chainsaw because it was the year of sudden-oak-death syndrome and falling trees, and I needed to have control over something, anything, and I didn't know who I was anymore.

After the separation, I was homeschooling my fourth-grade daughter, and the two of us were going to yoga together. We needed things to do, it calmed us both down, and Aubrey (a pretty, fit, newly divorced mom friend I'd just met) needed the hours of training to get yoga certified. When my husband was in town, he came too; yoga was something we had practiced before the kids. This gave us a way to begin again. I was grateful to Aubrey for her role in bringing us closer.

One Tuesday after class, Aubrey said, "Hey, can you break away for a mom's night out? You and me?"

I joked, "Hmm . . . I've got 'matching socks' on my calendar." She insisted until I said yes. I drove home, glad I hadn't upended my life with a divorce like Aubrey, who was scrambling to support her kids. I appreciated my husband, despite his insistence that he need not apologize for "putting his hand in the cookie jar when he didn't even get a cookie." Though I resented the phrase, it meant no physical line had been crossed.

Still, it drove me nuts to hear him say it, sitting across from our couples counselor, who had come highly recommended by my therapist. She thought, as a vet, the counselor would resonate with my husband's military background. Three sessions in, we learned the counselor was studying to be a veterinarian. But by then, we really liked Fred. He pointed things out that made sense: Pregnant or nursing kids for ten years, I'd given up our bed—hadn't I noticed my husband had retreated to the man shed with his Valiant comic books, his cabinets of GI Joes? Next, Fred got us to make a list of things we did for one another. When my husband read his list back to me—the time in sixth grade when he scratched all thirteen letters of my last name into the back of his hand, the thirteen poems he wrote on our last anniversary—I reread the poems, took him back, and vowed to try to "keep him interested," as one of my childhood male friends advised, though I was too exhausted raising our three kids to begin to figure out what that meant and resented the advice implying I was at fault, as if attraction and love weren't reciprocal mysteries to nurture.

Aubrey called that weekend about our mom's night out: a free hotel room in San Francisco. It sounded too good to be true—a friend I could trust, a chance to feel pretty again. I pictured steak, margaritas, time to troubleshoot the husband. I ransacked my closet, full of neck-high ankle-length floral dresses from momhood, all smelling faintly of lavender, playground skirts with the 100 dime-sized mirrors, tops with nursing slits. My best friend loaned me red earrings to go with the only outfit of mine she approved of, a red dress with black spiderweb lace and a worn pair of black tap-dance shoes. "You're not bringing that," she said, "right?" She was pointing to my canvas handbag with teddy bears embroidered on the outside, a diaper bag I'd converted to a purse. She kissed me on the top of my head. "Drink a margarita for me!"

But I couldn't leave behind the teddy-bear bag, with its many nested pockets big enough to hold my tarot cards. I pictured Aubrey and me in PJs, mugs of hot chocolate, throwing cards together. Facials after. I held on to this picture even as the night began to spiral out of control. Aubrey called ten minutes before I was set to pick her up. Actually, she'd meet me at the hotel. She was going to drive down with a friend.

I ran with it. I saw three of us sitting on my double bed, throwing tarot cards. Why not? The phone rang again. Could I pick up her other friend? Did I mind sharing a room with her instead of Aubrey?

Was this really the mom's night out for me? I voiced my fears to my husband while the kids fought over the "pretty chair." "Live a little, honey," he said, "and if you get wild, take pictures." I wanted to be the person he thought I could be, wanted to let go. He hugged me. "Have fun, honey—just come home to me." I left to the sight of my daughter chasing her brother, fork held high, pretty chair knocked over.

Aubrey's friend got in my car in a strapless sheer blouse, smelling of gardenia. "Did you mean to bring this?" she said, grabbing my bag by the handles. "Darling little bears," she said, and tossed it behind us. She shed her sexy sandals, resting manicured toes on the dash. "Do you mind if my husband crashes with us?" she asked. "He'll roll in around 3:00 a.m. I promise he won't get in your bed." No, I muttered, of course not.

When she spent the drive on the phone with Aubrey, I realized I'd been invited mostly to chauffer. It began to rain as we crossed the Golden Gate Bridge. "Wait," she ordered, "Don't go to the hotel . . . stop in the Haight." We pulled up to Aubrey hanging on the arm of a boy ten years younger than us. Cute, but young enough to be one of the kids I taught in my English class at the junior college. What were we doing outside of a tiny shop, window stocked with rows of feather boas? Why was Aubrey perusing fake eyelashes and leather halter tops?

"We"—Aubrey leaned in to hug me—"are going to a rave on Treasure Island!" Her bare shoulder left an arc of gold against my sweater. I blinked, stared up into the sky, rain beading my eyelashes. Treasure Island? That uninhabited—but for a warehouse or two— island in the bay? I began to feel alarmed. Could I back out?

Aubrey introduced the boy on her arm as Sky. He leaned in for a hug, his knit alpaca hat grazing my cheek, and said, "You're nervous. What are you afraid of?" Was it so obvious that I'd never been to a rave? I would rather go home and fight over the pretty chair with my kids. Was I really giving up already? *You can do this*, I told myself. I asked Sky where he was going to school, and sure enough, he was taking classes at the junior college. Mercifully, he'd already satisfied his English requirements.

When we got to the hotel suite, the door opened to a cluster of strangers, fresh fruit, champagne, hairspray. Aubrey disappeared into the adjoining suite, returned in a thong, and demanded, "Honey, let's get you dressed."

"But," I said, looking down, "I am dressed."

Her sidekick, aka Neal Young, now wearing a vest, leaned in and whispered, "It's your turn to have some." He meant whatever everyone else had ingested in the next room. The vision of earnest girl heart-to-hearts faded. I was in over my head. His dark-blue cotton pants, cinched at the ankles, ballooned out as he kneeled beside my chair. "If you're having a panic attack, I can get you a pill. Come with us! You won't regret it!"

Was this high school? I had no intention of taking a taxi with them to Treasure Island. My resolve solidified when Aubrey fell into my lap, giggling, and said, "You know, I would never bed your hot husband." So left field. So raw. She smelled like cinnamon. I began to pray. Wasn't the last six months of marital stress enough? Was Aubrey my friend, or a threat? I didn't make it this far in my marriage just to pass out at a rave. Even if that wild side was something my husband would love to see me express.

"I'm going to hold down the fort," I said. It worked. When the door closed behind them, I made a cup of tea. They emerged fourteen stories below, glitter-dusted bare legs and plumes of feathers trailing as they flagged down a taxi. Still, I felt deeply sad. *Hey wallflower,* I said to myself, *what's wrong with you?*

I crawled into bed fully clothed and fell asleep. At 3:00 a.m., the door burst open and they poured in, smelling of cloves and Bacardi. They turned on the lights, rustled into my bed, said, "Let us do your makeup . . . you could be so pretty!" Like *Midsummer Night's Dream* fairies. "Let us dress you!" Held up one filmy negligee after another. No, I said, no. I acquiesced only to a bit of eye shadow, a tiara on my head. I broke free to stand in front of the mirror. I met my own gaze, briefly, but it was enough: I didn't mind the glittering crown. But the rest was just not me. I missed my kids, my chainsaw, my husband.

And the little voice—the one that fought for me to stay alone at the hotel—said, *You can turn this around.* So, we weren't two friends having hot chocolate. There were four women and three men on my bed. "Let's do this," I said. I don't know what they thought I might do, but I took out the teddy-bear bag and fanned out the tarot cards like a barrier.

I pointed to the young buck, Sky, and said, "You first." He listened, stunned silent by the card he drew, the only male card in that round feminist deck: Pan with flute, loved and trusted by children, wearing a vest, alpaca hat, yoga pants cinched like Sky's at the ankles. The deck never fails when the reader shows up. "Wow," he finally said, "that's me!" Next, he drew the Trickster, a woman hiding under a coyote pelt who stands for the part of us that needs to be tricked into growing, talking, like the cards do, about all of us in that room, trading garments, trying on lives. So, I'd been tricked by an innocent invite. But it was worth knowing in exchange that I am not, nor will I ever be, a rave kind of girl. I am simply a one-man, one teddy-bear bag, heart-to-heart girl.

REWRITING MEMORIES

LAUREN HALSTED

When my daughter was born, I named her after my sister. Not her first name, that would have been too constant a reminder, but her middle. Audrey Lindsey Burroughs, after my sister Lindsey.

Just after Audrey's fourth birthday, I tried to tell her where her middle name came from. I can't say it was my best moment as a parent.

We sat in her bubble-gum-pink room, playing with her baby owl and baby seal stuffed animals. Out of nowhere I asked her, "Do you know what your middle name is?" I doubt she had even heard the term "middle name" before, let alone that she had one.

"No," she responded, without looking up from her stuffies.

I realized I should probably explain. "A lot of times, people have more than one name. My whole name is Lauren Marie Halsted."

She looked at me, confused. Silent.

"Marie is my middle name. And you have one too." I tried to sound excited, like Santa coming on Christmas morning.

Still, no reaction.

I probably sounded like background noise to her, like the *blah blah blah* in the Charlie Brown cartoons. She must have been thinking something similar to *Baby Seal is soooo cute and needs to kiss Baby Owl right now.*

Unfazed, I continued, "And your middle name is extra special."

Audrey looked at me, confused and skeptical, but I got a look. A small victory.

"It really is," I continued. "You were named after your Aunt Lindsey."

The moment I said her name aloud, I heard my voice crack and felt tears well up in my eyes. No heaves or sobs, just a constant stream of tears, like a springtime river bursting with the pressure of melting snow that had been building all winter.

"Mommy, why are you crying?" Audrey asked.

I wiped the tears with my hands, then shook them away with a wave, a gesture I inherited from my mom, something I had seen her do many times—usually minus the tears—when she didn't want to talk about something. A shake that said, *Don't worry about it.* Instead of saying anything further, I scooped Audrey into my arms and squeezed her tight.

"Mommy, you're hurting me."

"Sorry, honey. I just love you so much." I loosened my grip, and she found a comfortable place on my lap. It had been over twenty years— yes, two zero—since my sister passed away, and I was still physically unable to speak about her.

"I have an Aunt—what was the name?"

"Lindsey," I said, combing her hair with my fingers. "Yes, you do." I wanted to tell her everything about my sister—her warmth, her energy. But every time an image would pop into my mind, I felt as if I would drown in sadness.

The two of us sat there—Audrey in my arms, me completely unable to tell my daughter the stories that mattered the most. I kissed the top of her head.

***

Fifteen years before Audrey was born, my sister Lindsey was killed in a car accident. It was summer break; Lindsey was fifteen years old, and I had just graduated high school. Lindsey had a boyfriend whose family owned a cabin in Colorado, and my dad agreed to chaperone them on a road trip from where we lived in Southern California to the cabin.

Just outside of Las Vegas, my dad, Lindsey, her boyfriend, and two friends were driving through the desert, and the tire of their Suburban blew out. They were traveling at eighty miles per hour, and the tire's explosion was so fierce that it caused the car to flip over. My sister and her boyfriend were in the very back of the car, lying down without seat belts on. When the car flipped in the air and landed on the freeway, the back doors flew open. My sister was thrown out.

The doctors said that she didn't weigh enough to survive the impact. She hit the ground, and her spirit, or whatever our life force is called, was knocked out of her body. She didn't suffer. She wasn't in any pain. Which is something I should be grateful for.

When everything stopped moving, my dad rushed to my sister's body. He sat with her on the side of the road, stroking her bloody hair. A nurse happened to be driving by and she stopped, trying to help. They waited for an ambulance helicopter, which air-lifted her to the nearest hospital. The doctors tried for hours to save her. But it was too late.

When all this happened, I was at work at a coffee shop. My mom called me. "There's been an accident. You need to come home now." Her voice cracked as she hung up.

My mom didn't say what had happened. In the absence of information, my mind raced with possibilities. *Was Lindsey hurt? Was my dad okay?* I felt that something was wrong, really wrong, but I blocked that thought from my mind.

As I waited for someone to replace me at work, I cleaned up the shop, trying to distract myself. One of our regulars could tell something was wrong and asked, "Everything okay?"

"My sister was just in a car accident."

"I'm sure she's okay. People usually are."

Somehow, I knew she wasn't. I tried to smile at the customer, but it took all my strength to keep from breaking down in tears.

My suspicions were confirmed when I pulled into our driveway. Just before me, I saw the priest walking into our house. I heard my mom wailing upstairs before I saw her. I don't remember talking to her, or who told me what had happened. I think it was a good family friend wrapping her arms around me and whispering, "I'm so sorry."

The next few weeks were a blur of uneaten casseroles from well-meaning neighbors, funeral preparations, and my mom's body on the couch.

One thing I do remember is lying on the floor in my bedroom, unable to do anything but sob until there was no breath left in my body. Until my insides were empty. The only thing left was grief. I remember thinking, *Once I stop being sad about this, she will really be gone. Once I stop crying about her, I will have nothing left.* And since that sadness was all I thought I had left of my sister, I clung to it, my knuckles white from the force.

***

I clung to that sadness for twenty years. Even after all that time, I couldn't speak Lindsey's name without tears streaming down my face. *What was there to talk about?* It was a horrible accident. Of course, I was sad. Everyone was sad. I didn't think there was any other way to be.

But as I sat there with my daughter Audrey, I realized that my sadness over Lindsey's accident was preventing me from celebrating the memory of her. There was so much more to her life than that one horrible event, and I wanted to remember the beautiful things about her. The life that she lived, even though it was cut short. I wanted to share her with my children so they could at least somewhat know the aunt they would never meet.

I began with a picture, one I have framed and hanging on my wall. Lindsey has a huge, beaming smile that shows the depths to which she enjoyed living. Her hair is like a lion's mane, big and wild, dancing in the sun. Her neck and wrists are adorned in layers of beads and silver. She is stunning.

This is how I want to remember her. This is how I want Audrey to know her. I sit down next to Audrey and say, "Let me tell you a story about your Aunt Lindsey."

HOT SKINS

DEBORAH RUDELL

"What do you think, Tosh? Is it stealing to take this?" I asked my partner, Tosh, already feeling guilty.

Walking through the abandoned townhouse that last day, I had checked rooms and closets. Everything was empty, save for one last item, a portable sewing machine in the cupboard under the stairs. My roommate Chariya's. Had she forgotten it when she left? There was no one to ask and no one to give it to. I dragged it into the hall.

Tosh knelt and opened the white plastic cover. It was a Singer, almost new. After refastening the case, he looked up at me and smiled. "You just got a present, sweetheart; I know you'll be able to use it."

It was December 1985 in Rajneeshpuram, Oregon, the infamous "sex" cult that Tosh and I had been part of for the last three and a half years. I was twenty-eight, and my life was in chaos. Four months before, Sheela, the head of the commune, and her group of Ranch leaders had fled in the middle of the night. Bhagwan, our guru, did the same thing at the end of October. His plane was intercepted in the eastern states; federal agents had arrested and imprisoned him. The media had been all over it, creating a negative public backlash.

"What do you think, Gandi? Time for us to leave too?" Tosh had asked me, a few days previously.

"Yes, but what'll we do?" I'd never thought our spiritual community would end, so I didn't have a Plan B. And of course, that was part of the spell of the place. We could all be free to be in the moment, leaving the regular cares of the world at the commune gates. Now those cares were crashing through the gates every day with accusations of bioterrorism, wiretapping, and murder. And in response, there was a steady stream of vehicles winding their way along the twenty miles of muddy road, out the gates and back to another reality.

Of the ten thousand people that had been on the Ranch during the summer, only a thousand disciples remained. We had been living a life of unity and cooperation, our purpose to establish a precedent for a sustainable world. In less than two months, the smooth routines of the highly functioning commune had fallen apart. Where the focus on spiritual connection had been, daily life was now pointless and empty.

Tosh and I had gotten up early that last morning, unable to sleep, thinking about the journey we were about to embark upon. Dread filled me like water filling my lungs. I battled my mind to find some semblance of calm, while letting in the reality that the Ranch was finished. And with it, the dream of an integrated spiritual life vanished, like Aladdin's genie back into his lamp.

What am I going to do? How will I support myself? Was giving up my life, my money, my family and children all for nothing?

It was clear to me now that being with a spiritual teacher in Oregon had not worked. I was just an ordinary person, and a material life was all there was. I had learned my lesson. No more communes, no more gurus, no more groups. It was all a sham. My heart ached. Is this really all there is? Just what I can see and touch and hear? Is there really no God, no spiritual path or home for my soul?

As the van jolted along the rutted road, I thought about the sewing machine wedged in the back. The knots in my belly relaxed, but only slightly. Would I be able to sew again?

***

What am I doing? I asked myself a month later, as I nervously walked into the high-end fitness spa in Beverly Hills. I was with Trish, my colleague, tall, slim, and fit. Her long steps skimmed across the parking lot.

"I think this is it," Trish said, as she energetically pulled open the towering glass door. I followed her lithe figure.

"I'm here to talk with your manager," she announced confidently to the professionally dressed young woman behind the welcoming desk. Hardly noticing Trish, the receptionist's heavily made-up eyes stared, my attire shocking even her.

Her unabashed gaze snapped my attention back to my role in this marketing plan. Damn, this is weird. Self-consciousness flooded through me, flushing my face and chest. Despite the coolness of the air conditioning, I felt sweat slipping down the back of my bare arms and dripping off my elbows. While I was fully clothed, the unitard I was wearing was form-fitting Lycra and lace, not exactly absorbent. Like my change in lifestyle, my outer expression with my clothes was a far cry from the unisex down jackets, jeans, and work boots I'd worn for the last three years. Why did I ever agree to do this?

Just then, a strikingly attractive man burst into the room, his well-developed muscles exuding testosterone. I could feel his practiced eyes arrogantly taking in the package I presented. I wanted to disappear. I was consciously using my body and beauty for commerce. Somehow, cutting and sewing these remarkable outfits was a lot more fun than I was having at this moment. Stay focused on selling the exercise wear. Disassociate yourself from the predatory staring. It's just the outfit, not you, I told myself. Yeah, right.

"Hello ladies, how can we help you today?" His voice was deep, resonant, his eyes scanning my entire body.

Trish stepped forward and extended her hand, "Trish, from Hot Skins Exercise Wear, and this is my model, Gandi." I nodded briefly in his direction and quickly looked off to the side to avoid his stare.

While the Ranch had been an arena for open sexuality, it was a sensuality connected to the heart, mutual attraction, and honesty. This was entirely different, about being an object, about luring in the man for my own purpose. I needed to make money and thought sewing was a solution, wanting to avoid the dancing and spanking porn movies my friends were making for a living. Sewing was harmonious with my idea of who I was, but I never dreamed it would bring me to this moment.

Reluctantly shifting his gaze to Trish, the man perfunctorily took her hand and responded automatically, "Josh, owner of Beverly Hills Top Star Fitness."

After seating himself behind an enormous desk of glass and stainless steel, he rolled his leather chair back and looked up expectantly. Trish pulled out oversized glossy photos of her exercise wear and explained how well suited this designer clothing line was to his exclusive fitness spa.

Somehow, I found myself standing beside his chair. My bare foot was traveling through the air, arching over his lap, landing lightly on top of his desk, directly in front of him, demonstrating how flexible the bodysuit was. The rush of life force was intoxicating as I gently, deliberately placed a hand on my hip, showing off the leg line that extended to the armpit. There was full coverage of the important parts, breasts and groin, yet the outfit revealed tanned skin through the lace on the torso, over the hip, and all the way down to my ankle. As I lifted my shoulder-length hair, carelessly flipping it back, the power of my sensuality filled me.

"The outfits are all manufactured right here in California, and I'm happy to take your order for this exclusive line today," Trish concluded.

I lowered my leg and casually walked toward the door to give him a full view of the back. My buttocks prickled, feeling his lust. As I veered to the side, I allowed myself to look out the window into the garden of a large courtyard. Reflected in the glass I saw papers exchanging hands between Trish and Mr. Testosterone. The "show" idea was a success, despite my inexperience with modeling. Bhagwan had said the strongest force in our lives was our sexuality, and it was part of everything we do. Little had I known until that moment how right he was.

After three years of isolation and communal living, after three years of giving away all decision-making to a guru and then wondering how in the world we would support ourselves, it was a simple sewing machine found in the back of a closet that brought me back into the world.

DIAGNOSIS

JENNIFER GASNER

Growing up in the 1980s, my reputation was as "the girl who always smiled." It was the sole compliment that I accepted with gratitude, not skepticism, that made me feel pretty and lovable. My other nickname, Klutz, emerged along the way. That label frustrated me, but I found a way to integrate the two. I laughed off my bloopers, blaming my blond hair and bulky glasses. Making fun of myself before others did became a way of maintaining my image.

I always seemed to be experiencing random falls and injuries. My list of blunders included a broken arm, a head-over-heels sail off my bike, and countless disasters resulting in broken glasses.

In eighth grade, I was diagnosed with scoliosis. I went to the doctor for an evaluation of my curved spine, and my mom informed him about my habitual falling.

"She just has weak ankles—nothing to worry about," he assured us, after a cursory examination.

My family and I accepted that explanation.

During my sophomore year, I felt a shift in my body. I had trouble walking in a straight line, my penmanship became illegible, and my perfected cartwheel abandoned me.

At sixteen, I began my year of painful tests and worry. *What is really going on with me—am I going to get sick?* I wanted more of an explanation for my growing instability. At the same time, I never thought my diagnosis would be serious. I kept smiling, avoiding the subject of my doctor visits with my friends.

The night before my senior year began, Mom and I sat in our living room. She was in the wingback chair, entranced by *People* magazine. I lounged on the plaid couch across the room, soaking in my last night of no homework.

Three weeks prior, we had visited a neurologist at Children's Hospital. Dr. Jaradeh, a specialist we were referred to, repeated the tests my local doctor had done.

The phone rang, and Mom scurried across the burnt-orange carpet of our living/dining room to reach the tan handset. I watched with halfhearted interest. After Mom's greeting, she looked at me, surprised. I sat straight up like a meerkat at attention, with wide eyes on the lookout for a friend or foe.

Is it the doctor with news about my tests? Do I want to know?

Mom rustled through a pile of mail and found pen and paper. She pulled out a chair from the kitchen table. She sat on the olive pleather cushion and mouthed the words, "Dr. Jaradeh."

My heart leaped in anticipation of the verdict that this man of medicine had about my clumsiness. I followed Mom's end of the conversation, frozen in my spot—as if the carpet was a sea of snakes, waiting to strike.

Mom muttered a lot of "uh-huhs" followed by furious writing on the small bit of stationery. She asked for spellings of words yet did not repeat anything for my attentive ears to pick up. My mind jumped back and forth, matching my increasing heartbeat. *It's nothing . . . it's something . . . it's nothing.*

The clock marked ten snail-like minutes. I heard, "Thank you," and Mom went to place the handset on the wall. With her back to me, she let out a sigh. She turned around and gave me a reassuring smile. "Well, you want to hear?"

What the hell do you think? "Lay it on me."

I jumped up from the couch to check out Mom's notes. I stood behind her, glancing over her shoulder.

The words "Friedreich's ataxia" and "muscular dystrophy" jumped out. The saliva in my mouth vanished.

The image of a pitiful person in a wheelchair with a death sentence flashed before me. That's all I knew about muscular dystrophy (MD).

I didn't fit the portrayal I saw during the annual Jerry Lewis Labor Day MD telethon. The twenty-two-hour star-studded event had been going on since the 1950s and raised millions of dollars for research and other services for people with types of MD—mostly children, aka Jerry's Kids.

As I continued to look over her shoulder at the notes, I saw my case fell into the minor category; I took it to mean MD was something inconvenient that I'd have to contend with occasionally. *Mild. That means I am not like Jerry's Kids.*

I realized I used to joke about being a Jerry's Kid because my dad's name was Jerry. Is this a self-fulfilling prophecy?

Despite my confusion, as time went on, I felt settled for the first time in months. We had an answer. Sure, it turned out to be something I had never considered and knew nothing about, beyond the Labor Day telethon. But that wasn't me. It couldn't be me.

That following weekend, my friends and I went to a football game. I decided to dump the news on them. I laughed about being a Jerry's Kid. I became gleeful—skipping up the bleachers, smiling, and singing—*I'm a Jerry's Kid.* My friends looked at me, perplexed, wondering why I wasn't acting devastated. I ignored their worried eyes and scrunched up faces. I felt I could let nothing dampen my smile.

A few days later, the calendar proclaimed Labor Day. This year, I had reason to watch the annual telethon.

"Mom, will you watch it with me?"

As confident as I felt, knowing my mild case would not be represented—and that the kids with the most severe disabilities would be in the spotlight—something still told me to avoid watching it alone.

"Sure," she said, putting on a brave face.

Outside the expansive window in our living room, streams of water blurred the glass. The sky looked dark gray and ominous. The visual torrent mirrored the uneasiness I felt within. Mom and I sank into our couch, watching our thirteen-inch screen glow as Jerry Lewis did everything to elicit tears and money. The dreary light from outside matched with the pitiful tone from the TV.

As I had expected, I couldn't relate to a single example of MD on the screen. I am not one of them; my case is mild. Soon, the national telecast cut to its hourly update on the local station's efforts. The news anchors who dished out the daily dose of news sat in a semicircle in front of a dull-light-blue background. A teenaged, lanky, somewhat disheveled, glasses-wearing boy in a wheelchair appeared in the middle, miserable in his gray ensemble. He slouched and seemed to be leaning to one side. His spectacles were greasy, and his face looked gaunt. When he spoke, his voice slurred. The female reporter said his name was Jason.

As Jason spoke, I picked up the same copy of *People* that Mom had been studying days earlier. I dove into the cover story, Patrick Swayze. I looked up when I heard, "Jason has Friedreich's ataxia."

I dropped the magazine, and my hand covered my mouth. My eyes darted to Mom, hoping she'd tell me I misheard. "Oh, no," she proclaimed, as she searched my face.

I fled Mom's watchful eye, sped down the hall to our small beige bathroom, and slammed the door. My back leaned on the door while muffled tears streamed down my face. *This is not happening. Please, God, no.*

To make matters worse, or maybe better, I expected two friends any minute. My meltdown had to be quick, and they could not see a trace of it on my face. I let myself take a few final deep sobs. Then I stepped to the sink, stared at my reflection in the mirror, and shook my head. My surroundings seemed to melt away as I focused all my attention on my shocked wet face.

I rubbed my eyes free of any evidence and opened the door. The room where the TV took up space appeared empty. A shot of relief came over me when I didn't see Mom waiting to console me.

The doorbell rang. I wiped my frown and replaced it with a bogus smile.

My dream to be a radio or TV personality—occupations where being well-spoken and engaging were important— shattered. It felt like the last seventeen years of my life had been erased, and I had to start over from the beginning to find out who I was.

As an adult, I can see how initially I continued my jovial façade in public to mask my private grief. But after a visit to an MD support group, a room full of people whose smiles seemed to have vanished, I decided I did not want to live angry at the world and sad for myself. I chose to be the girl who smiled to find joy in the new part of her life.

Now, thirty years later, I use a wheelchair. In many ways, I am the same girl: a smiley klutz. But my twenty-five years in a wheelchair has taught me happiness does not depend on my ability to walk or talk. I wish I could tell that seventeen-year-old girl that Friedreich's ataxia would make me the fierce woman I am. I wish I could tell that seventeen-year-old that she will move to California without her family, have a boyfriend, and lead a deeply fulfilling life, pursuing her dream to be a writer.

NOT FINE AT ALL

ANASTASIA ZADEIK

A phone is ringing.

Waking to a shimmer of predawn light, I realize it's the landline next to my bed, and my heartbeat quickens, my ribcage contracts. Calls at this hour always bring bad news. *My parents. My in-laws.* I glance at my husband of twelve years, Tom, who is still asleep, breathing heavily. I reach for the handset, hoping my two young children have also slept through the noise.

"Hello?" I say quietly.

"Stacy?" I do not recognize the voice. "It's Jon, Tessa's brother."

My brain plays catch up. *Jon. My husband's ex-brother-in-law. Tom's ex-wife Tessa's brother. A man I've never met or spoken to. Ever. Something must have happened to Tessa. Or, oh god, Tom's daughter, my fifteen-year-old stepdaughter.*

"Is Ally okay?" I ask.

"Yes, Ally's fine," Jon answers quickly, emphatically. "It's not Ally. It's . . . It's . . . Shit, this is harder than I thought it would be." He sounds defeated. No, wounded. It must be the cancer. My husband's ex-wife, Tessa, Jon's sister, has ovarian cancer. Or uterine cancer. Or ovarian cancer that has spread to her uterus. It's not entirely clear.

With my hand over the mouthpiece, I hold the phone out to Tom's still-sleeping form. "Honey," I say. "It's Jon Pittman," adding rather unnecessarily, "Tessa's brother."

Tom does not respond. There is no love lost between my husband and his ex-wife's family. Tom's first marriage was ill-fated; he and his first wife, Tessa, barely spoke on their honeymoon and fought incessantly thereafter. The union lasted eighteen months, just long enough to develop deep-seated hatred for one another and bring a child into the world. Ally lived with her parents for only five days—five days—before they separated, and from the start, Tessa embraced the archetypal crazy ex-wife role: mercurial, irrational, spiteful.

"Tom," I say, a bit louder. "It's your ex-brother-in-law, Jon."

I hear Jon's voice, "Stacy? Stacy?" and lift the handset back to my ear. "Ally's told me you're calm," he says. "Reasonable. It might be easier for me to talk to you, if that's okay."

"Allllright," I respond slowly, sensing a trap. "But Tom's right here if you change your mind."

"Yeah, okay," Jon says. He repeats, "okay," as if to himself. "Listen, no one knows I'm calling you. And no one will be happy when they find out." He pauses. "But the situation is untenable with Tessa and Ally living at my mom's. We need Ally to be out of the house."

"Wait, what?" I say. "I thought you said Ally was fine. Did she do something?"

"She *is* fine, and no, she didn't do anything. It isn't about her. Not really, but—" Jon sighs. "I don't know where to start." Another pause. "This morning, Tessa came back to my mom's at 3:00 a.m., wasted, with these two huge guys, and they started taking things. The stereo, the TV . . ." Jon's voice trails off.

"I see," I say, reflexively, though I don't see at all. "And Ally was there?"

"She was asleep," Jon says. "Down the hall. But my mom woke up and came out. The guys said Tessa owed them money, so my mom confronted her, and Tessa started screaming, 'My husband won't let you treat me this way,' which is odd, you know, since she's not married."

"Right," I say, my voice rising; I'm thinking the fact Tessa is not married is the least odd thing about this story thus far. "And?"

"And . . ." There is another pause, long enough for me to wonder if Jon has hung up. When his voice returns, his tone is ominous. "Stacy, there's just so much you don't know." Pressure builds in my chest and abdomen, dread settling in. I sit up and lean against the headboard. It doesn't help. Jon goes on, talking fast: "Tessa is an alcoholic, an addict, for years, using cocaine, heroin—"

"Wait. Hold on," I say, sitting fully upright, trying to keep up. "Did you say heroin?"

Tom rolls toward me, rubbing his face. "Heroin?" he asks. "Ally's using heroin?"

I turn to him. Cover the mouthpiece. "No," I say. "It's Tessa." Words tumble out, a tangled repetition of what I've just heard. As I say, "She brought men into Kit's house at three in the morning and they started taking stuff—" Jon interrupts me.

"Stacy, wait," he says. "There's more . . . more than the alcohol and drugs." He begins telling me a story I can scarcely follow. Tessa's been in and out of jail, rehab, and psych hospitals—*for years*. They've tried everything, he says. Initially, doctors said it was schizoaffective disorder, but the most recent diagnosis is bipolar, and the new medications clearly aren't working. It's only getting worse.

As this man I've never met unravels the past, my thoughts tumble the way my words did earlier: *Schizoaffective disorder? Jail? Psych hospitals? Years?* Memories of Tessa's behaviors flood in, exposed in a totally new light: the vitriol-filled letters to Tom's parents and colleagues; the furious rants and totally meritless accusations of kidnapping or assault; last-minute cancellations of visits; unexplained absences when we arrived to pick up Ally; constant moving in and out of apartments; Ally's half-packed suitcases missing critical items like a winter coat or underwear. The clouding-over of Ally's face whenever we asked about her mother.

I'm reeling, but also aware of how overwhelming Tessa's cancer diagnosis must have been to all of them. "Oh my god," I say. "And then she got cancer, on top of all of this?"

"Cancer?" Jon says. His tone stops my breath. "Wait, Tessa told you she has cancer?" A second goes by, maybe two. My stomach falls into an abyss. "Stacy, Tessa doesn't have cancer."

"Tessa doesn't have cancer," I repeat, turning to share this bombshell with Tom. Heat rises up through my torso, into my head. I feel nauseated. *No cancer?*

Two years ago, Tessa called Tom's sister, Jill, who was fighting stage-four breast cancer at the time, and after swearing Jill to secrecy, Tessa told her she had ovarian cancer. Ally didn't know, and she, Tessa, didn't want us to know either. After agonizing about withholding this critical information from us, Jill called Tom, and for months Tom and I struggled to navigate being supportive of Ally without revealing to her the nature of our concern. Hours, days, weeks were absorbed by discussions about how to handle the situation with grace and compassion. Meanwhile, Tessa and her mom, Kit, gave the cancer as an excuse for extended absences on Tessa's part. "Chemo," Kit would tell Tom. "A new experimental treatment. Another surgery."

Then, the past summer, Tessa called and talked to my dad, who was visiting and happened to answer the phone. Weeping, she told my dad she had uterine cancer, less than a year to live, and didn't know how to tell Ally. My father spoke with Tessa for almost an hour, comforting her, and then he told Tom and me that we had to discuss the cancer with Ally. So, we did. We outlined what we knew and told her we hoped her mom would beat it but, if something were to happen, we would be there for her. We all cried. Hugged. And it was all a lie. There was no cancer. *No cancer.*

"Stacy?" Tom reaches for the phone. I tilt away, lift my hand in the universal stop sign.

"Sorry. I'm trying to understand, Jon. You're saying Tessa doesn't have ovarian *or* uterine cancer?" While everything he is telling me is shocking, I cannot wrap my head around someone lying about having cancer, particularly to Tom's sister, whose life has been defined by a fight against it. To me, this is incomprehensible. Beyond spiteful. *Cruel.*

"No, she definitely does not have cancer."

The phone is out of my hand.

"Jon, are you serious?" Tom says. "Tessa doesn't have cancer?"

There is a pause as Jon gives an answer I cannot hear. I gesture to Tom, move my head toward his. He tips the handset. "Tessa's clearly delusional," Jon is saying. "I mean, she says she's talked to Jesus, one-on-one, in person. She's whacked out, violent. That's what's landed her in jail a bunch of times. We just don't know where the behavior comes from: the drugs, the illness, the ECT—"

Tom looks at me, bewildered. I whisper, "Electroconvulsive shock therapy."

"Shock therapy?" Tom says. "What the hell?"

"I know," Jon says. "It's a lot. But the bottom line is, you need to come get Ally. My mom can't kick Tessa out as long as Ally's here, and my mom's seventy-five, Tom. I'm worried about what could happen to her with Tessa bringing men into the house."

Perhaps because it brings out my mother-bear tendencies, this last comment infuriates me. *Jon is worried about his mom? What about Ally, his fifteen-year-old niece, asleep in her bedroom down the hall?* This sets off a chain reaction of combustible emotions: disbelief, remorse, fear. *This has been going on for years? How could they not tell us? How could we have missed it? Who's looking out for Ally?*

"What about Ally?" I ask.

"Ally?" Jon's voice registers surprise. "Ally's fine. She's got school, her friends."

She's fine? I think. *How is that possible?*

"What about all this other stuff," Tom says. "Does she know about all of it?"

"Yeah, she does," Jon says, then repeats slowly, "she does," as if he's realizing what this could mean, the repercussions. The collateral damage. "She knows all of it."

And it occurs to me, Tessa and her mother, Kit, lied about the cancer, but so did Ally. *The whole time, Ally had another option—a stable home with us. Tom, me, two younger siblings that adored her. If she didn't want that option then, why would she want it now?*

"You've got to understand," Jon says. "Ally is all Tessa has. Without her, there'd be no reason for Tessa to get well. My mom thought if you knew, you'd try to take Ally away."

About this, Jon is right. We would have, and within minutes, Tom has agreed to do just that. He will fly to Washington, DC, and take Ally out of her grandmother's house. He will bring his fifteen-year-old daughter—his angry, accustomed to chaos, teetering at the edge of addiction and mental illness, totally not-fine fifteen-year-old daughter—to live with us full-time.

With one predawn call, the collateral damage spreads.

RADIANT IN RED

MARIJKE MCCANDLESS

She stepped out of the shower, wearing a thick terry-cloth robe, her hair wrapped turban-style in an old towel.

"How do I look?" she asked, prancing.

"Radiant," he said.

As the mother of the radiant one, I couldn't help but smile. Hmm. This guy has potential. Here was someone who appreciated simple raw natural beauty, no glamour strings attached.

Or should I say no ropes.

Our twenty-three-year-old daughter, Sanni, had just begun seeing a new man, Alex, and this was essentially their third date—sharing our family Christmas 2015 at a Mammoth Mountain condo. His schedule was busy, and they were geographically challenged. She lived in Seattle, and he, well, he lived in a van, mostly in California and Nevada. Mammoth was in between.

They had caught each other's attention at a book event—his book signing, to be clear. She had just given up on online dating, vowing instead to approach the next "cute" guy she saw. Lucky him. She stood in line with a friend, then smiled, tossed him her business card, and dashed out the door.

Alex called her and something clicked between them.

When I first met him, I knew almost nothing about him other than that he lived in a van, liked to rock climb, and had written a memoir about it. Pretty early on, I learned he had a nonprofit foundation that supplied solar power to needy people. Impressive.

Others around me worried. Didn't I care that he lived in a van? Didn't I care that he wasn't living a traditional life? Didn't I care that he was a crazy rock climber?

No, not really.

Our family is an outdoorsy adventurous bunch. Heck, when the kids were four and seven, and my husband Jay and I were staving off a midlife crisis, we moved our family to a remote fishing village in Mexico. There, we homeschooled our kids while living in a thatched roof palapa with hanging beds and deadly scorpions.

No. I really didn't care that Alex lived in a van, or that others called him a "dirtbag climber." I didn't even mind that he had chosen a life of climbing over finishing his college education.

I got it.

Jay and I had been down nontraditional paths ourselves. We had driven from Washington State to the Yucatan peninsula in an old Datsun pickup one summer and hiked 450 miles up the coast from San Francisco to Oregon another. Then there was our "Palapa in Yelapa" phase with our little kids. Later we began taking three to four weeks off a year to meditate, and we started rock climbing at fifty-three. Most of our peers had long thought we were crazy.

So, no, I didn't mind that this new man in our youngest daughter's life led a nontraditional life. What I cared more about was whether he and my daughter complemented, inspired, and enjoyed each other. Did they get each other? Did they make each other smile?

Of course, I didn't know a lot about Alex when we first met. For instance, I didn't know he was a world-famous free solo (i.e., ropeless) climber. And I didn't know that a documentary crew was tracking him while he trained for an impossible feat up a 3000-foot wall in Yosemite.

I'd never been to Yosemite Valley itself—just to nearby Tuolumne the summer Jay and I met. We were not rock climbers back then, only romantic fools in love. We went on an off-trail hike and ended scrambling up a rock wall looking for a view. On the way down, however, I froze, just fifteen feet from the ground, terrified of falling, suddenly aware of the inherent danger. It took an hour for Jay to talk me down the wall, inch by sweat-soaked inch. But that was long ago. Now, I love rock climbing. The ropes help.

In the beginning, it was unclear how Sanni and Alex's new relationship would develop, especially considering the physical distance between them and his unusual lifestyle. We watched, bemused, as the two got to know each other by meeting for weekend rock-climbing forays that grew longer with each passing month until finally she moved in (to his van) with him. They traveled widely, climbing together, spending a summer in Europe, another in Wyoming, traveling to Morocco, and spending every spring and fall in "the valley"—Yosemite, that is.

We, too, got to know Alex. Every few months, the two of them would go out of their way to make an opening for "family time." We played games, cooked, ate, and climbed together. He got along well with the whole family.

Early on, just after they met, we all went climbing in Index, Washington. On that fated day, Jay and I loaned Alex our rope, which, unbeknownst to us, was too short for the climb. The rope slipped through the end of the belay device and he fell about ten feet. He hurt himself pretty badly (compression fractures to his spine) and could barely walk. We were all scarred from witnessing his fall. Two days later, though, he flew to China. Turns out he was meeting up with another climber to take on Corazón de Ensueño, one of the most difficult multipitch routes in the world. When we saw what Alex climbed shortly after that fall, it began to sink in what an extraordinary—not to mention committed and passionate—rock climber he was.

We wondered about the effect of that fall on their brand-new relationship. They did too, but after waffling briefly, they stuck it out together—eager to complement each other's lives, despite the challenges.

We'd hear tiny rumors about a movie being made about Alex's rock-climbing life, but no details. We heard other rumors that he was working on a "big project." The biggest thing we could think of was El Capitan in Yosemite; it's the most impressive rock wall in America, maybe the world. Was he planning to climb El Capitan without ropes? But we didn't ask or focus on that thought—too scary.

Eventually, Sanni commented about a film crew hanging around and filming her, too.

"Before," she said, "they hadn't been interested in me. But now, they've started doing little interviews with me and filming us at all different times and places, even in the van."

We didn't think too much about that either, except that it sounded stressful and we worried a bit how a film crew might impact their budding relationship.

In late fall 2016, Jay and I joined Sanni and Alex in the valley. We'd heard Alex had fallen a couple weeks earlier and sprained his ankle, which was still swollen and bruised. I offered castor-oil compresses and was pleased to see the swelling decrease. Nonetheless, I couldn't believe he was walking and climbing on it. Ouch. Not too much later, I asked Sanni how his "project" was coming along.

"Oh," she said nonchalantly, "he tried, but bailed, saying it didn't feel right."

Her low-key attitude reassured me, and his response sounded level-headed. At least he wasn't going to climb if things were not aligning.

In spring 2017, we joined them for a couple days back in the valley. The unspoken understanding was that Alex was continuing to train for his "big project." We still didn't know for sure what his project was, though El Cap seemed a good guess. The film crew didn't want word getting out. In hindsight, I could understand that.

Some weeks later, when we were back home, Sanni called us, sobbing.

"I had to leave," she cried. "I need to give him space to do his thing. It was so hard to leave."

Our daughter's distress was visceral. Outwardly, I quickly donned my be-supportive-without-interfering parental cap and tried to comfort her without asking prying questions. But inwardly, my stomach turned over. I was terrified. Was Alex climbing El Cap? My body relived my own experience of being frozen fifteen feet above the ground that time in Tuolumne. Was Alex climbing the sheer rock wall of El Cap—a granite face that stretched more than 250 stories into the sky—with nothing to catch him if he fell? Unfathomable.

On the call, it was clear Sanni was facing her own mountainous challenge: supporting and loving Alex meant leaving him unencumbered by her presence to do his thing. That's hard.

As a mother, though I feared for both of them, I trusted her emotional intelligence. Sanni loved and respected this man; she would not impede on his dreams. I was proud of her. My own challenge was staying focused and supportive of her, not fearful and worried.

Days later, before the news was officially out, she called us, crying again, but not in sadness. "He did it. He free-soloed El Cap!"

In the fall, we were invited to the LA premiere of *Free Solo*. One of the National Geographic staff hugged me and whispered, "Wait until you see it. Your daughter is the heart of the film."

For me, the pinnacle of the film was not the scaling of El Cap, but the moment when relationship-shy Alex called Sanni from the top, saying for all the world to hear, "I love you!"

A few months later, a friend texted me: "Holy guacamole. Was *Free Solo* just nominated for an Oscar?"

Shortly after, we watched Helen Mirren and Jason Momoa at the Oscar award ceremony make the announcement for best documentary: "And, the Oscar goes to . . . *Free Solo*." The directors, producers, and Alex Honnold got up on the stage, and right next to Alex—professionally made up, coiffed and absolutely radiant in her red-carpet-worthy red dress—was our daughter Sanni, whom the director specially thanked for her role in making the film "not boring."

I gotta say, I didn't see that coming.

Alex climbing El Capitan without ropes? Maybe. Sanni and Alex moving to Tanzania and living in tents? Maybe that as well.

But I never imagined that the love shared by these two, a dirtbag climber and the "girl next door"—a love that blossomed in the mountains despite cramped living quarters, tense emotional situations, and physical injuries—would in three short years launch them to the upper echelon of *Hollywood*—the Oscars.

Nope.

I definitely didn't see that coming.

THE LOST FIELDS OF SORIA

NANCY G. VILLALOBOS

It was a quiet revelation, really. My response to the small arrow-shaped sign that flashed by the train window went unnoticed by the other passengers en route to Madrid, including my daughter Rocío on the seat beside me. Even if she'd been awake, she mightn't have seen the way my eyebrows raised or felt the sudden quickening of my pulse or heard the sharp intake of breath. If she had, she might have asked, "What's going on, Mom?" but she didn't.

Segovia had not been our original destination. I'd wanted to take the AVE, the famous bullet train, to the faraway southern city of Seville, where Rocío had spent a college semester, but when we arrived at Atocha, Madrid's cavernous train station, all the seats for Seville were booked. Our time was limited, so we needed a closer destination. "How about Segovia, Mom? The Roman aqueduct, the Alcázar?" At my nod, my third child took charge. She flipped through my thick guidebook, whipped out her mobile phone, and booked us a room on the first try. As we boarded the slower, regional train for Segovia, I applauded the way she'd abandoned the stagnant job market in Los Angeles and elected to pursue her fledgling graphic design career in Madrid.

Rocío, the only one of my four children to share my love of reading, likewise was the only one to have the ojos claros, the hazel eyes that resulted from the genetic mix of my Anglo-Saxon blue and the deep mestizo brown of her father's. Tito, my Peruvian husband, was also responsible for her iconic Spanish name. Contrary to what most Spaniards she met assumed, she was not named for la virgen del Rocío, but for my husband's favorite pop singer in the early '70s. I was glad we'd decided to spend this last weekend of my visit traveling together before I returned to California.

Once aboard and settled, soothed by piped-in classical music and lulled by the train's rhythmic movement, I reached into my bag and pulled out one of the poetry anthologies. Thirty years earlier, when I'd developed a romantic affinity for España and her literature as a university student, I'd collected Spanish poetry anthologies. But between time and one intercontinental move and another, the beloved Spanish poetry anthologies had disappeared. Now in Spain for the first time, I had hurried to replace a few in the very land that had inspired the writing.

Settling back in the seat, I slipped a hand into my shoulder bag and pulled out a slim anthology, the one that included five classic Spanish poets. I turned immediately to Federico García Lorca and his "Canción del Jinete." Even on this modern train in broad daylight so many years later, his words transported me in an instant:

Córdoba,
Lejana y sola . . .

Córdoba,
Distant and lonely . . .

The sixteen short lines took me back to the romantic university student I was, entranced by the image of the melancholy horseman riding resolutely forward on a valiant black steed, olives in his saddlebag, on a deserted highway under a full moon, knowing full well that death awaits him before arriving in Córdoba. Leaving the familiar words of Lorca, I turned to "Campos de Soria" by Antonio Machado. I'd never heard of Machado or any fields of Soria, but his impressions of life in an impoverished area of rural Spain captivated me. As I read, I kept returning to the description of a farmer plowing his autumn field behind a pair of plodding oxen. Swinging from the heavy yoke between the black tousled heads is a willow basket—the cradle of a babe. The mother follows behind her straining husband, scattering seeds into the furrowed earth. I'd felt that need to tend to a child and get the work done at the same time. I wanted to know more about the land he so poignantly described—Soria—wherever it was.

When the train finally pulled out of the urban Metro tunnels and into the countryside, I interrupted my poetry reading, drawn by the view. It had rained all week in Madrid, but here the winter sun shone bravely on huddled villages and fallow fields. From inside the cozy and overheated coach, I watched the landscape grow steadily bleaker, turning into a collage of gray soil, dusty olive groves, and silver hills— much like the images from Machado's poems.

Arriving and settling into our charming room in the hotel pushed all thoughts of poetry from my mind, but from our small balcony, I could see the ancient city wall and the stark and unforgiving landscape of Castilla y León that stretched beyond. Rocío and I set out to find the city's claim to historic fame, the aqueduct, using only the local city guide provided by the hotel. We discovered a small art museum tucked away in a hidden plaza and were quietly thrilled to find a unique collection of early works by Pablo Picasso, our favorite painter. Later, we indulged in flaky pastries from a nearby bakery and then strolled around the Plaza Mayor, electing to skip the interior of the famous cathedral and shop for ceramic souvenirs instead.

Late in the afternoon, with our purchases tucked in a shopping bag, we wandered arm-in-arm along more twisty cobbled streets until suddenly, around a corner, the two-thousand-year-old Roman aqueduct, the sightseeing objective of our day, rose a hundred feet into the sky, stretching over the city as far as we could see. The late-afternoon photograph I took of Rocío that day in front of those arches is one of my favorites. Her petite, slender form and the high-wattage smile that got her on the cheer squad always makes me wonder why people say this beautiful young woman looks like me.

It wasn't until that evening as we sat reading in the lounge that I looked more carefully at the guía de la ciudad, the city guide I'd been carrying around all day, and saw—in miniscule print near the bottom of the list of sites of interest—that number fourteen was the casa-museo of Antonio Machado, poet. We'd passed it that afternoon, according to the map, between the Picasso exhibition and the pastries.

The terse description of the pensión where Machado lived for a time and the adjoining small museum with some furniture and personal objects didn't sound interesting enough to consider altering our plan for the next day. Had I read the length of his occupancy more carefully, I might have reconsidered.

The snow began at breakfast. Lovely, wet, lacy flakes floated down on the ancient walled city and its visitors, turning us into ghosts as we walked. We were the only visitors that frigid morning in the historic and drafty citadel known as the Alcázar, rumored to be an inspiration for Sleeping Beauty's castle in Disneyland. We fantasized about residing in the damp chambers as Rocío, the family photog, aimed her lens at gilded ceilings, coronation portraits, and me. *This is as relaxed as I've seen her. It must be the first break she's had from the stresses of resumé writing and job hunting. I won't mention the Machado museum.*

The snow had turned to a cold and dreary drizzle when we boarded the train for Madrid. Once settled, I opened my thick guidebook to see what it had to say about the place we were leaving. I hadn't consulted it since our serendipitous decision to pick Segovia over Seville as a destination. I had read only a few paragraphs before I came to the words, *the poet Antonio Machado did most of his writing in Segovia and nearby Soria.* The air went out of me with a deep sigh. The tiny museum I'd deemed not worthy of visiting could have been a place of discovery. I could have perhaps photographed Machado's writing materials, caressed his books, peered through his reading glasses. I might have spent time with his poet's spirit and opened my soul to his inspiration.

It's the traveler's regret, I reflected, *the roads not taken, the sights not seen.* But as travelers, we make those choices. Antonio Machado was dead, and my beautiful daughter was alive. His voice lived on in my anthologies, but I didn't know how long it would be before I'd see Rocío and her smile again. Passing up a visit to a musty museum seemed a worthy trade-off for the magical morning we'd spent together in a deserted Spanish castle on a snowy December day. And the mysterious fields of Soria, as close as they might be, would still be there if I ever chose to return.

Resigned, I stowed the travel guide and picked up the poetry anthology, opened to Machado's poems. Leaning back in my seat, I lifted my gaze to the train window just as a small, arrow-shaped sign flashed past: SORIA. The sharp intake of breath, the sudden quickening of pulse, happened then. In my lap the anthology lay open, my finger marking a random verse.

¡Oh, sí! Conmigo vais, campos de Soria! . . .
me habéis llegado al alma,
¿o acaso estabais en el fondo de ella?

Oh, yes! You go with me, fields of Soria . . .
You have touched my soul,
Or were you, perhaps, always in its depths?

LOST AND FOUND

HEATHER M. BERBERET

I'm in fourth grade, walking to Candalaria Elementary School in Salem, Oregon. It's drizzling rain, like always, and I'm thinking about the books I'll write when I get older, if only I could figure out what to write. Well, I'm only nine. I'm pretty sure I'll know some stories when I get older. Definitely by sixth grade.

I am thirty-seven years old, sitting in a wheelchair next to our day-old daughter. She lies on a table in the NICU, a cannula pushing air into her lungs. Yesterday, at only thirty-five weeks pregnant, I sat at a booth in Jimmy Carter's Mexican Restaurant, sacrilegiously eating a cheeseburger, when I felt a gentle "swoosh" between my legs. I prayed it was simply a strange, pregnancy-related bladder problem, but a trip to the bathroom ruled that out. So, I paid the check, waddled back to my office round the corner, leaking amniotic fluid the entire way, and called my OB/GYN. After seventeen hours of Pitocin-driven labor, my daughter rushed into the world, surfing a wave of desire, hope, blood, and more amnionic fluid. Her birth went fine. It wasn't until afterward that everything went off the rails.

She retracted when she breathed; her chest compressed, rather than expanded, when she tried to take a breath. Imagine a straw that collapses when you try to draw-up your Coke Zero. I held her for only a few minutes before they whisked her away. My wife went with her while I stayed behind, waiting for my placenta to deliver. When it didn't, emergency surgery followed, and I lost a lot of blood. And now I'm here, so weak I can't stand on my own, watching our baby struggle to breathe. I wasn't any more ready to deliver her than she was to be born. I want to touch her, hold her, but she is so small and fragile, I'm afraid I'll hurt her. She belongs inside of me, putting on weight and strengthening her lungs, rather than lying alone in a plastic box, naked under bright lights, covered in tubes and tape.

She will come home after nine grueling, terrifying days, small, but breathing and nursing on her own.

I am forty-two, sitting in my car after walking our daughter to her first day of kindergarten. We've had five years of constant togetherness, and now she is ready to take her first steps toward an independent life. I'm bereft. Mothering reshaped me as I pivoted away from myself, let go of projects and commitments, and wrapped myself around her. And inevitably, her sparkling baby magic seduced me into wanting another child. I tried for a long time, but miscarriages followed all my conceptions. Now, I am tired and too old. So, rather than turning toward another child, as I've watched so many of my friends do, I use the grind of a parent's life to distract me from my secondary infertility. Parenting, work, parenting, sleep, rinse, repeat.

Five months later, as I lie next to my daughter as she fights the highest fever of her life, my mother lies in intensive care, brain-dead from a stroke. Tomorrow morning, we will tell the doctors to turn off the machines, remove the tubes, and allow her body to grow still.

I am torn. I want to go be with my mother on her final night alive, even though she won't know I'm there. But my baby is sick and needs me to hold her, comfort her in the way only I can. My gut pulls in two directions, as if rubbery cords of blood and flesh still bind me to them both.

If I go to my mother, hold her hand in the dim light of the ICU while the monitors beep softly and the life-sustaining oxygen swooshes in and out of her lungs, can I fix things between us? If I tell her that I'm sorry that I focused only on the bad between us, could our cord, fragile and frayed, be repaired? Could our intermingled cells find each other and reattach, remembering their original form? She can't change; her life is over. But can I?

My daughter holds my hand against her burning cheek while she sleeps. If I leave her, will she suffer more? Will she call out for me?

What if her fever rises even higher, requiring a rush to urgent care, and I'm not there to hold her and tell her it's going to be OK?

Finally, I choose to mother rather than be mothered, but the choice will haunt me. I turn forty-three six days later.

I am forty-seven, sitting at our dining room table, eating Easter dinner with my wife, our daughter, and my dad. It's a perfect San Diego spring day—warm gentle breezes, soft sunshine, and baby-blue skies. Earlier, we had dug out, from deep in the back of my kitchen cupboard, the Easter Bunny cake mold my mom used when I was little. It makes two cakes, each half of a sitting rabbit. Baked and placed together with a massive amount of frosting, they make a three-dimensional rabbit. Covered in coconut fur with jelly-bean eyes, it sits in the middle of the table, in all its lopsided glory. I have to look around it as Dad and I talk about how difficult it was for me to turn forty-seven.

Forty-seven feels like a death sentence. Mom and Grandma both died at sixty-seven, so my evil, depressed self had taken to whispering, "You've only got twenty years left, you know. Is this all your life is going to be?" My heart feels flat in my chest, my shoulders stuck and weighed down. I am simultaneously Sisyphus and the boulder, trapped in a repetitive, futile loop of joyless struggle.

Oh, the irony of being a clinical psychologist and totally oblivious to the causes of my own depression.

I don't tell anyone I've given up hope that my life could change. It's too vulnerable, too pathetic. As a privileged, upper-middle class, highly educated, white woman, the world caters to me. Already cringe-worthy in my mind, I have no desire to hear my hopelessness spoken out loud, that I have somehow, in all of my lost chances, lost myself.

So instead, I whine about turning forty-seven.

"You're only forty-six, you know," my Dad says, interrupting me. "You won't be forty-seven for ten months."

I laugh.

"I know how old I am, Dad."

I've always known more than my father.

"Well, so do I," he replies, sounding annoyed. "I was there."

That surprises me. Embarrassed, I blurt out, "OK . . . Just . . . just talk about something else."

I suck at calendar math, so I grab my phone, surreptitiously holding it under the dining room table while I search for a "How Old Am I?" app, which I find. Apparently, I'm not the first person to forget their age.

And then, after just a few taps of my thumb, the numbers "46" appear on the screen. These few pixels of light, glowing under a plate of glass, change everything. It doesn't matter that it's a trick of my consciousness; a bolt of lightning shatters that damn boulder. I step away from the shards of stone and am lifted, out of my darkness, into the gentle California sunlight.

I am forty-six. Really forty-six. Asleep in my bed, I dream about becoming a polar bear. As I morph from human to animal, I experience an expansion of self, then a freeing of my mind and a deep connectedness with my body. All therapists know that dreams are the mind's way of processing experience, So, as my muscles effortlessly drive me across snow-covered tundra, while a bitterly cold wind filled with ice crystals whips through my thick, bristling fur, I know that it's *more* than a dream. It's a telegram from my unconscious mind to my conscious self.

I wake up, and I decide that my life isn't set in stone, defined by what I've lost. I've been given a do-over year; it's time to dig down deep, take some risks, and find a fuller self than the one I've been living.

I am fifty years old, sitting in a ratty but comfortable chair in the back of a Barnes & Noble, editing the trilogy I began writing four years ago. As time has passed, I've found that the more I write, the lighter and freer I feel, like I've floated free of Earth's gravity and have the entire universe to explore. I write about a woman who loses herself and her family through addiction. Then one morning she wakes up naked and alone in the woods. To find her way home, she must accept her entire self: the human, who plans for the future but becomes desperate and hopeless when things don't work out as she wanted; and the animal, who acts on instinct and lives in the joy of the moment.

And then, after she works that out, she saves the universe.

SUSHI

CHLOE SPARACINO

I get a haircut from Sami at Bamboo Salon in Hillcrest and learn all about Scorpios and smoking pot because Sami's dad is a Scorpio, and her ex-husband is a drug addict. She does not know a lot about weed but she knows more about it than I do. Growing up in a religious home meant that drugs and astrology were sinful and made God angry. But now that I am choosing my own way, I want to learn about the outside world. Sami tells me that people smoke weed to relax, and that Scorpios like their girls to be ladies.

"That's me! I'm a lady." I peek at her from behind a row of wet bangs.

"You're right up their alley. Speaking of Scorpios, are you going to see Seth today?"

"Probably."

I decide to get a manicure and a pedicure, and I feel gorgeous.

I ride over to Seth's shop with the excuse that my bike has been making a grinding noise.

Seth's bike shop is a two-room blue house with white trim that has been converted into a retail store. Other than a large painted sign that says Bike Shop hanging over the door, and the bicycles lining the front of the sidewalk, his store could easily be mistaken for a home. Seth's shoulders are slumped from exhaustion, but his face brightens when he sees me.

"How is your day going?" I smile and look away quickly because he is so handsome.

Seth pushes his black baseball cap up off his forehead. His hands are covered in grease from working on repairs all day. When he takes a swig from a tall can of Arizona Iced Tea, I can see his thick black hair curls a little at the base of his neck. I find it hard not to stare at him; his deep brown eyes are as magnetic as his voice.

I met Seth two months ago when I walked into his shop to buy a bike. I stop by as much as I can, not only because I enjoy his company, but because I appreciate how his expertise has helped me start my new hobby of biking instead of driving. He runs the busy shop all by himself and is open with me about whatever is on his mind. Lately, I have been wondering if he is interested in me beyond just the friendship.

"I gave all day and I need to be filled back up. This shop is not about the money and buying and selling—though that is a part of it. This shop is a revolution, a new way to live. I want people to care about themselves, care about the environment, and live a better life, and give up being ego-driven and money-hungry. I want my customers to feel like they are a part of this shop and be invested in creating something new with me."

As Seth explains his vision, I think about how he treats me like a partner, not like a child, the way my ex-husband John treated me.

Like when it was pouring rain outside and I was going to visit a friend in the hospital. John wanted me to go to Home Depot to pick up a part for him instead.

"No." I stood my ground, shaking on the inside, with my hand on the front doorknob.

"Fuck you. I hope you get in an accident. And if you do, don't call me. I won't come help you."

I shake my head to erase the memory. The smell of rubber tires brings me back to the bike shop.

"Ever since I started riding a bike instead of driving a car, I feel healthier and happier. What you are doing in the community is price-less." I watch the light come back into Seth's tired eyes.

Seth lifts my bike into the repair stand, asking me questions about where the noise is coming from. Turns out there is nothing wrong with my bike except I am shifting gears incorrectly. I blush deep red. He tries not to laugh, but he is smiling from ear to ear. He thoroughly explains how bicycle gears work then picks up the shop phone when it starts ringing.

＊＊

I remember hosting a dinner party for John's friends, Greg and his wife Lori. After dessert, I cleared the table and began loading the dinner plates in the dishwasher.

"You know what you do when your dishwasher breaks?" John asked.

"What?" Greg replied, grinning as if he already knew the joke.

"You slap her."

Every muscle in my body tensed in shame. "John!" I scolded.

"Come on. It's funny." He waved me away like mosquito.

＊＊

Seth hangs up the phone and clears his throat.

"I think it's cool that you care about learning the right way to do things," he says softly.

I beam at him. He tugs at the bottom of his T-shirt like he is restless to get something off his chest. He looks into my eyes, and I feel like I am a maze that he wants to untangle.

"You want to grab dinner? I'm about to close up the shop."

"Sure, that sounds great!"

My armpits sweat from nervousness. We have never gone to dinner before, and I hope this means he likes me more than just as a customer. This might even be a date.

He reaches behind a display of bike locks to switch off the neon OPEN sign on the front window. He hits the shop lights and locks the front door. "I should probably warn you that I showered today but I'm really stinky. I wear the same clothes several days in a row, I have grease stains on all my jeans, and there is no structure to my days or my life. Sometimes I still feel like I am a little kid, still waiting to grow up. I live on Mexican food and snacks from 7-Eleven. I don't eat, maybe just once a day, and I'm losing weight, noticeably, and people are asking me about it. This is my life right here, this shop. I'm here to provide a place for people to understand themselves and enjoy the outdoors. Bikes tell you about yourself, like the way you describe horses, and when I'm working on someone's bike, I want them to be in the room with me with all their energy, otherwise it is not worth it to me to work on their bike. Having them here brings up a lot of spiritual things for me, and I have the most amazing conversations with my customers every day . . ."

He continues talking about energy, spending time outdoors, and books he has read. I attempt to contribute to the conversation, but he does not stop talking. I grow hungrier as the evening sky grows darker. My hypoglycemia is kicking in.

"I am going to wait outside so you can finish getting ready." I start to walk away.

He quickly comes back to the present and reaches for his keys. "Do you like sushi?"

* * *

In the truck, he continues his monologue, and I bring up his conversation style. He says his friends just tell him to shut up, while others have told him they feel like they are drowning in a verbal flood.

"Yeah, I feel like I am drowning."

"I have underdeveloped social skills," he confesses, hunching his shoulders like he wants to disappear.

"I want to contribute to the conversation, but I feel I'm like watching a movie, because there is no interaction. It's just you, talking."

"You do contribute! You say things that give me all these ideas and connections, like when you asked me to show you how to shift gears properly. It reminded me how great it feels when someone comes into the shop and wants to learn. How I find different ways to solve problems and new ways of understanding and explaining them . . ."

He keeps talking and parks the truck. Sapporo, the sushi restaurant, is painted black on the outside with red trim. Inside the front door is a glass case of raw fish. Seth talks to the greeter and she leads us to a table in the corner of the crowded dining room. Seth pulls out a chair for me to sit next to him so we can sit close.

We do not look at the menus because he is telling a story about how he has used words to attack, how he is not proud of it, and how it relates to his dad. He starts describing a verbal fight he got into once. I break eye contact as the room is turning into quicksand.

"I'm doing it again, the talking without stopping."

I am not really listening or seeing Seth anymore. The sushi restaurant has disappeared and is replaced with open highway. When I left John two years ago, I drove across the country from Michigan to go live with my parents in Los Angeles. Tears had muted my throat, but by the time I reached Texas, I started yelling at the windshield.

"How dare you treat me like that! I will not put up with this anymore."

My freedom felt dangerous and glorious. I got to stop when I wanted to stop, and eat when I was hungry. I pulled off the highway for rest stops, McDonald's, gas stations, every hour on the hour, just to prove it. No more starving from hunger until I fall asleep from a total lack of energy, and no more holding my bladder until my kidneys cramp up in pain.

"I can't do this. I have to go." I pick up my purse and stand up. Seth's eyes widen. The server runs over and asks if she can bring us some water.

"No thanks, I have to go."

I walk out of the restaurant. The minute I hit outside air, I gulp fresh oxygen. I walk across the street and order Thai food to go, wolfing down pad Thai as I walk three miles home. Feeling like I have been trapped underwater, my fiery lungs yearning to breathe, now I have broken triumphantly to the surface.

HIMSELF

SARAH VOSBURGH

He just *sits* there.

Such a *beast*.

With a mono-expression, his dark eyes unblinking.

Urgent eyes thrust against the morning, waiting to be acknowledged—

an acknowledgment he will predictably and disdainfully rebuff.

He sits tall, proud, groomed, ready for the world,

waiting and watching for fault as I begin morning ablutions and preparations,

judging my moves, my efficiency, my haste, or lack of it.

Waiting on misstep so he can leap away in exaggerated disappointment,

a low growl in his throat.

I misstep now just so he'll leave, having learned not to care, for my own sake.

That morning glare, for the past decade.

That glare, that icy smooth censuring glare,

is a searing spotlight in the day's beginning that should be gentle and full of promise.

I know he will be in surveillance mode when I leave the bedroom.

Sitting in a position of repose, melting into the sofa,

all liquid and languid and stretched so casually with practiced abandon,

he cannot admit fondness, appreciation, hooded eyes now—

those shrouded telltale windows to his soul.

Breakfast prepared while he breathes in and out in easy rhythm.

In and out like a yoga master, as though all the world assumes his pace.

Except those of us who serve him, of course, scurrying to obey implicit demands.

Never once does he glance in my direction.

One does not watch the servants.

This would be an admission of anxiety, eagerness *We* do not express.

No, he will wait.

When he is called, he will stretch

and yawn,

and stretch again,

and saunter to his repast,

casting me aside to sit and enjoy in silence,

but for his chewing.

Chomping, smacking, squishing, clicking, chewing,

spewing bits here and there.

His bearing is regal,

his gait a smooth economy of movement.

No royalty here, as he would have you believe; his family tree is mixed,

varied as any sixth- or seventh-generation American.

His profile strong and proud—patrician, even,

reminiscent of generations of good breeding one might expect from a blue blood.

He's just lucky the genes combined when he was made

into the beautiful ginger he is,

full of rare elegance and profile and form and intelligence and freckles.

So much more than any other man could be in my life;

I'm graced with his love. A protective wrap.

This he sighs, throaty and warm in my ear, to convince me of his inherent superiority to my ilk.

He was at the head of the line when genes were handed out.

I got him. So lucky.

He got it all.

So he thinks,

and he thinks I don't know.

He thinks he can blame his infidelities and indifferent aggression on me.

He thinks I'll believe his unspoken untruths because he is who he is.

He thinks he's better than me and I am indebted to him.

He thinks his version of love will keep me from noticing, or calling him on, his insolence.

He thinks he has risen above.

But I *do* know—I know all.

The family history,

the anonymous father

mother of questionable breeding

sleeping in the streets

panhandling

sibs and children unknown

spread far and wide

volatile red-hot hissing anger

and the damned inelegant chewing.

He thinks I don't know.

And he thinks I won't notice or care he used the bottom of my husband's closet for his litter box this morning.

Ten years I've withered under his arrogance,

known and kept his veiled insecurities.

He has served me too in his own way,

assuring all manner of things shall be well with his embrace.

Always there are soothing murmurings against my fears and anxieties.

Lying in refuge, in communion, our hearts beating in concert,

or with his warmth pressing against my aching back or singing knee.

TERROR ON INTERSTATE 5

ALLAN E. MUSTERER

What is he looking for? Why is he leaning down to the floor?

Those were my only thoughts as Dave, a close friend and fellow minister, and I sat in the back seat of a fast-moving car with three strangers—one of whom was frantically searching under his car seat. It was early in December of 1978 on a cold winter's night in a desolate area of Interstate 5. Just a few hours earlier, our car had broken down as we made our way along the empty road.

Dave and I, along with two other minister friends, Jim and Bill, were traveling home following a funeral of another minister. We had made the long drive to comfort his wife.

I was driving the first leg in Jim's diesel Oldsmobile. A dense fog blanketed the highway. A few cars and semi tractor-trailers joined us as we all cautiously headed southward.

Thirty miles in, the engine began to act strangely, struggling with intermittent power. We stopped at the first service station we saw and were told the nearest diesel mechanic was 150 miles away. It was 10:00 p.m., so Jim decided, "Let's go for it," and he took over the driving, hoping the engine could last.

It wasn't but a half hour later that the engine seized and stopped. I felt my body tense as I braced for an impact. Jim put the car in neutral and we coasted off the road, onto the shoulder, and then into the dirt. Endless farmland lined both sides of the freeway. The open fields were bordered by barbed-wire fences. Large balls of tumbleweed littered the landscape. It was eerily desolate, and we were officially stranded.

At first, I was not concerned. Surely, someone will stop and give us a ride to the next exit where a tow truck could be called. Standing on the road's shoulder, we attempted to flag down a few passing cars, but to no avail. It was freezing cold, and the fog was growing denser by the minute. As we tried to signal a few more cars that sped by, we looked at one another with worry.

What are we going to do if no one stops? We had no water, food, or warm clothes. With the engine broken, we had no heat for the night, and in the 1970s, there were no phones on the road to call for help. Within a few minutes, though, a light-blue Monte Carlo came screeching to a halt, bypassing our position by a good thirty yards. It kicked up a huge cloud of dust.

The car backed up and stopped adjacent to our car. We all heaved a sigh of relief. We thanked God that someone had the courage to help us. Three young, clean-cut men emerged from the Monte Carlo. They greeted us, offering to fix our car.

"The engine has seized, so we need a tow truck," Jim said.

"We're happy to take one or two of you to the next exit to make that call," the Monte Carlo's driver said. Relief flooded my body as Dave and I volunteered to go with them.

The Monte Carlo was a two-door coupe. One man entered the back seat, followed by me in the middle and Dave behind the front passenger's seat, and we drove off. Based on the appearance of the three young strangers—tall and physically fit—I thought they might be basketball players from nearby Fresno State University. The driver, bigger than the other two, did all of the talking. The man in the passenger seat stared ahead, not saying a word.

I attempted to make conversation:

"Boy, we really appreciate you guys picking us up."

"Where you guys coming from?"

"Do you live near here? Where are you headed?"

I was met with silence.

Suddenly, the atmosphere in the car changed. Any sense of being safe evaporated as the stranger in the front passenger seat bent down to retrieve something. The air all around us turned frigid as gut-wrenching fear engulfed me. He came up holding a double-barrel sawed-off shotgun. Swiftly, he swung it around, placing the barrels inches from my face.

"This is a stick up!"

As I looked down the barrels of that gun, I realized that my life might end in that moment. I silently prayed, as I wondered what God was doing. Images flashed through my mind: My loving wife decorating our new home. Our smiling, precious little boy. Driving to work with the top down in my little red sports car. The joy of serving as a minister in a small local mission. Dinners with my parents. Summer vacations at a beach house in Baja, where I taught my son to fish.

I silently asked, "Is this all You want of me, God? Or is there more You want me to do?"

The gunman seemed to be nervous, his grip shaking. I feared the gun would go off unintentionally. I began to speak.

"My name is Allan. You don't have to do this. Is there a way we can talk this through?"

Angered, the driver slammed on the brakes and yelled, "Shut up!"

The car skidded off the road, sliding across the shoulder into the dirt in a cloud of dust. As soon as the car came to a stop, the driver turned toward me, his face contorted in a vicious grimace. He grabbed my throat, pushed me up against the rear window and screamed, "If you don't shut up, we will kill you right now!"

"Okay," I said.

The driver demanded we give them all our money, including our wallets, keys, and watches. I quickly handed everything over but hesitated when handing over my key chain with irreplaceable sentimental attachments: my wife's high school ring, a small gold knife, and gifts for being the best man at two weddings.

The man in the backseat next to me counted the cash. The driver warned us, "If you don't have enough cash, you're going to be shot."

The man next to me said, "It's only sixty-five dollars."

"That's not enough!" the driver yelled. The gunman opened his door, and with shotgun in hand, commanded us to get out.

"Walk to the barbed-wire fence. Don't look back. You don't want to know when the shots are fired," said the gunman.

Slowly, Dave got out of the car. He took a few steps toward the fence just a few yards away. As I followed him, I noticed the gunman behind the door had the shotgun pointed down. This was our moment. When my feet hit the ground, Dave bolted toward the back of the car. Instantly, I followed. We ran as fast as we could, hurdling over three- and four-foot balls of tumbleweed littering the area.

The air felt like breathing razorblades. I feared the blast of the shotgun with every step. But it never came. Running about thirty yards, continuing to hurdle over one tumbleweed after another, I tripped over a large one and fell to the ground. Cautiously, I peered back toward the car through the tumbleweed. I saw the gunman break open his shotgun, pull out two shells, and toss them into the front seat. He jumped into the car and it sped off.

My body buzzed with adrenaline and I was grateful to be alive but worried the men in the Monte Carlo might come back. Dave and I quickly regrouped and attempted to flag down a car. Within minutes, a car pulled over and the driver offered us a ride to a nearby Denny's restaurant where we could call the police and get a tow truck for our stranded friends.

It was one in the morning when we entered the empty but warm restaurant. A waitress brought us a phone to call the police. As I hung up, the waitress returned with a burly tattooed man and said, "Here's Brett, your tow truck driver. He'll take good care of you."

We ordered a cup of coffee and waited for Brett to find the disabled car and our two friends. The police arrived, took our statement, and quickly left to pursue the perpetrators. Once we were reunited with our friends, Brett drove us to a nearby car dealership. At dawn, we left the car for repairs, got a rental car, and headed home. On the way home, we listened to the radio reporting a high-speed chase down I-5, pursuing three hijackers. After a long pursuit, the three men were apprehended and arrested. Eventually, they were all sent to prison for nine years.

When I made my way into my wife's arms that night, my heart began to calm. As I fell asleep that night, I reflected. I had reached out to God and put myself in His hands. I was preserved and, in the process, delivered a life-changing lesson. From that moment on, I live on grace-given time.

GREASING

EILEEN MATHENA

We are firemen. That's our navy rank and job. I'm Fireman Welch. Fireman Beckmann and the rest of us enlisted women work grueling hours down below in the engine rooms onboard the USS *Hunley*. And when we hear, "FIRE! FIRE! FIRE!" over the ship's announcement system, we drop tools or food, and we run. We run toward fires.

This time, it's not a fire I'm staring down. It's far worse.

It's Fireman Beckmann, and she is standing before her locker surrounded by white walls, white linoleum, and white sheets on bunks stacked three high. She's been "greased," and I know what I am seeing, and wish to God I wasn't.

Wearing a one-piece pink-and-white floral swimsuit, Beckmann is splotched here and there with oil and grease. She is crying. Pale-blond curls and shoulders shaking, she's hunched and quiet. She is trying desperately to remove the fouling with a small white boot-camp-issue bath towel. Mean black streaks spread so the grease is on her skin and the towel. I smell diesel and oil, she is drenched in it. My heartbeat rips at my chest.

It's 1984, and I am one of forty-two enlisted females in a crew of 900 sailors on the USS *Hunley* in Scotland. At twenty, I have been promoted to third-class petty officer, but my work life is miserable. It's full of harassment and hazing by my male counterparts in engineering, but I am determined that they will not get me.

As I look at Beckmann's bruised and grease-stained body, the anger rises; I can feel the heat on my neck. My ears pulse. A few days ago, a male fireman had told me, "Welch, it's *your* turn." I had made it clear: "Leave me alone, and I won't report you."

Since then, when I'm at work in the "pit," the name for the engine room, no one speaks to me. I write official entries in the logbook. There are crude drawings of men and women getting greased and notes of warning to those of us who refuse to participate. I am afraid and looking over my shoulder all of the time.

Greasing involves a grease gun and sodomy, a word I've never actually stated and know only from the Old Testament's Sodom and Gomorrah. Old information and new meet, and my thoughts race. Sodomy is against navy regulations.

A grease gun is a tool that injects heavy grease into critical equipment in my division. The grease guns are locked up, and only supervisors have keys. For women who participate in greasings, I don't doubt it involves rape as well sodomy.

I had overheard two senior female petty officers brag about their greasing and admit that "it was nothing," and "like sex." When I had confronted them, one laughed and said, "Oh, Eileen, you're too serious. This is an old tradition."

Looking at Beckmann, tears well up and I blink them away. This can't end well, narcing on these dirtbags. Who gave them the right? We all just want to do our jobs.

Quietly, I walk toward Beckmann; I don't want to startle her. When I am next to her, I say, "I'm so sorry this happened. We're going to get you some help, Becks."

I don't want Beckmann to talk. I know what they did to her. *I feel so old.*

I keep my voice down and whisper, "Becks, I've tried to stop this before. A few weeks back, I spoke with our department head and he said he'd look into my allegations, but nothing came of it." The chain of command has failed. Failed Beckmann and me and so many.

Trying to reassure her, I say, "It's going to be alright, Becks." Even though I don't believe that. It's not her fault, but the command—our leaders—will blame us anyway. Her eyes were all fear. Her whole body was shaking. I knew I couldn't let it slide this time.

Who will help us? No one in engineering. They'll side with the petty officers, write me up, and then sweep it all under a stairwell. The last time I had complained, the commanding officer lectured us females on "how to get along." *Maybe Senior Chief Coglin?* I respect and trust his authority.

"Beckmann, let's go to Senior Chief, he'll know how to help." I swallow. This doesn't get undone.

We leave the female berthing. The lighted passageways are empty. It's the hour between evening chow and the movie on the after-mess decks. We arrive at the senior chief's office. I knock on the gray metal door, and a third-class petty officer peers outside.

"We need to see Senior Chief Coglin," I say.

"He's in the chief's mess."

Keeping a protective arm hovering, I ask the young man to get Senior Chief. "Now would be good." The words feel like a growl, but I realize it's angry tears jammed in my throat. As the third-class hurries out, I catch the door, and we step inside.

I murmur reassurances to Beckmann while my self-doubt screams. Am I doing the right thing? I have no idea. A kid. She's JUST a kid. This is what they had done to others. No one—not one of them—came forward to stop it.

The metal door opens. "Fireman Welch. Congratulations on the promotion to third class," booms the senior chief.

His voice is a good match for this giant man with an oversized shiny bald head. He ducks under the top edge of the door. Dressed in his khaki uniform, he looks ready to start the day, even though it is nearly twenty-hundred hours (8:00 p.m.).

Senior Chief takes a look at Beckmann and says, "I'm going to make a phone call. When I return, Fireman Welch, we'll *talk*." He picks up the receiver on a black rotary phone and dials. Within minutes, a female corpsman from medical is at the door. Coglin excuses himself and, without touching Beckmann, he guides her out of the office.

My hands are damp, and I wipe the palms down the front of my dungarees. I stare up at the ceiling. I just want to sleep. I'm sad and so very tired.

Senior Chief returns, pulls two gray metal chairs out, and asks me to have a seat. He takes a yellow legal pad off a desk, finds a pen, clicks it, and sits down. This is the first sign from anyone in authority that they have an interest in what I have to say.

"Fireman Welch, you should have come to me first," says Senior Chief.

"Did you know?" I ask.

He takes a breath. "Rumors, but I needed firsthand knowledge."

"Senior Chief, I hoped it would get to you, but I had to report it to my chain of command first."

With a heavy heart, I pull a little green notebook out of my back right pocket and tell Senior Chief, "I don't have names and dates of when it happened to the other women. Just notes of threats to me. But if you get the engine room logbooks, the names and dates of the greasings are there."

He nods and says, "That's okay. I'll get the logbooks. But when did you first become aware of this hazing?"

"I think it started four or five months ago, when a supervisor had told me I'd have to *earn* my way into the pit. I didn't know what that meant until Fireman Mason showed me the logbooks full of notes and pictures about greasings. Mason said, 'participation is mandatory.' When I asked about the engine room supervisions, Mason just shook his head. That's when I knew they were running the show, so I went to the chaplain."

"Did things improve after you spoke with him?" Chief's calming voice gives me courage.

"No, it got worse. I stopped getting relieved from watches, got put on shore patrol, and was allowed little-to-no sleep for forty-eight to seventy-two hours at a clip." Tears drop to my shirt and I blink to shore up the rest.

"What exactly did the chaplain say?" Senior Chief asked.

"That he couldn't help. Seemed like he didn't care. He said, 'use the chain of command.' I had already done that. Engineering commander just sent me back to the pit."

***

As I spoke with Senior Chief that evening, I felt the first bit of hope I'd felt in months. I also realized how rare the man sitting in front of me truly was. I had gotten lucky—somebody heard me.

Senior Chief brought charges against nineteen sailors, all enlisted—yet no one in leadership faced any repercussions. Even he couldn't get them held accountable. I tried to bury these events, while carrying the burden of guilt for not having done enough to protect Beckmann and others.

Almost forty years later, my daughter, who had enlisted in the navy, shared with me that friends of hers working on ships in San Diego were still being greased.

DANCING HEARTS EMOJI

SUZANNE SPECTOR

Six months after my eightieth birthday, I stood in my kitchen, pouring my five o'clock glass of wine while chatting with my daughter Donna, who was visiting from Indiana. The phone rang and the answering machine announced my last name, Spector, so I picked up the receiver, thinking it was one of my other daughters. But the announcement continued: Jonah. I scanned the Spector file in my head. *Was there a Jonah Spector? Maybe some long-lost cousin of my ex-husband Myles?*

I answered the phone with a question mark. "Hello?"

It was a male voice with a New York accent. "Hello?" he responded, also with a question mark. "Wait, you're not my ex-wife Suzy."

"No," I laughed. "This is the OTHER Suzy Spector."

"WHAT!" he exclaimed. "There are TWO of you?"

"Yes. And we both used to live in Solana Beach."

"How do you know THAT?" he asked, incredulously.

As I walked into the front room to privately continue the conversation, Donna called out a warning. "Mom, stop giving away your identity." I shrugged her off, thinking, *Don't be paranoid. I know this man. He's New York Jewish.*

"Well," I told Jonah, "thirty-four years ago, my furniture arrived in Solana Beach from New York without a warning. I said to the moving guy, 'How could you just show up without calling me first?' 'Lady,' he replied. 'I did call, and your son said it was okay to make the delivery.' I told him, 'Guess what? I don't have a son!' He shook his head and replied, 'Well, ma'am, there's somebody named Suzanne Spector in the Solana Beach phone book who has a son.'

"So," I said to Jonah, "I guess that was YOUR son. But how come you called MY number? Don't you know your ex-wife's phone number?"

"No, we've been divorced for over thirty years. I needed my grandson's new address so I could send him a birthday check," Jonah continued. "Did you know the other Suzy Spector is a terrific artist?"

"I thought you were the artist."

"ME!" he exclaimed. "What do you know about ME?"

"Well, I lived in Solana Beach for ten years, and every place I went, they asked, 'Spector? Are you from Spector Design?' I assume that was your business."

"It was. I wrote a story about that. It's in my memoir. If you want to give me your email address, I'll send you the story."

As I recited my email address, Donna shouted from the other room, "Mom, your identity! Stop giving it away." I was intrigued that Jonah had written his memoir.

A few hours later, as soon as my daughter and I returned from dinner, I checked my iPad. *Just curious,* I said to myself. Sure enough, Jonah had already sent me an email. And thus, it began. We emailed so much that I became conditioned to the happy ping of *You've got mail.* After two weeks, he said, "We must meet. How about tomorrow?" I wondered if he'd be as much fun in person.

I told myself I was totally "cool" about getting together, but I tried on my entire summer maxi-dress collection the night before our date. I knew he liked bright colors, based on a photo he'd sent of his twenty pairs of colored sneakers. I chose my loudest dress—a bright-orchid sleeveless sheath, with all my lumps, bumps, and wrinkles on full display.

Even though I told myself it was just a casual meeting between two New York Jewish transplants, I arrived for lunch flustered and five minutes late. I saw him waiting in the entryway to Fidel's and, distracted by his bright-orange T-shirt, I scraped my fender as I pulled into a spot. I was asking myself, *Should we have stuck to email?*

But as we settled into a booth at Fidel's and started munching on chips and salsa, I relaxed and commented on the aboriginal art that covered the front of his shirt. We talked about travel and art and New

York bagels, about children and grandchildren and writing and tennis. He told me a sexual fantasy, and I told him one back. Did I really do that? We talked nonstop for almost three hours. And then, out of nowhere, he leaned forward and said, "I'd like to kiss you right now."

Without skipping a beat, I replied, "I'm really enjoying our connection, but I have to confess that my hormones aren't working anymore. They sure drove me when I was younger, but now, they're gone."

My disclaimer wasn't a deal-breaker, though. When we finally got up from the table to leave, he put his arm around me and gave me a little hug. It felt delicious. As I leaned into it, I thought, *Hmm, what's this about? I didn't know I had any juice left.*

***

He began signing his emails "love." I wasn't going there, so I signed mine with a yellow heart emoji. I'd never used emojis before, but they sure were handy. When he asked what that meant, I said, "Not stop or go, just yellow . . . but a heart."

I was loving this email romance. Sexual overtures were made by him and ignored by me. But on our third lunch date, he looked at me, his eyes full of warmth. "I've never met a woman like you. I think about you all the time. And I don't understand the mixed signals you're giving me by pulling away physically." Before I could sputter a reply, he leaned in and said, "I love you, and I don't understand why you're being so skittish about making love. At our age, we don't have time to waste."

"Well," I answered, "I'm afraid that if we started to share more physical closeness, you'd just be coming over, and we wouldn't be leaving the house much. I like to get out and do stuff."

He looked at me in disbelief. "We have so much in common, how could you possibly think that it would only be one thing?" I thought, *Oh my God. Is this really happening?*

I came home feeling floaty and warm. *This might be fun. I like this man. I'm going to just send him the heart emojis in every color without saying anything.* I opened my iPad, took a deep breath, and instead, I hit the vibrating heart emoji. To me, that said, *my heart is pounding.*

Then I wrote, "Okay, carpe diem," and signed it with the emoji of two dancing hearts. As I pushed the send button, my stomach flipped. I had dived in. I was scared and excited. I felt the walls protecting my self-sufficiency beginning to melt. After forty-plus years as a happy single woman, could I open myself to be loved?

Six weeks after the wrong-number phone call, we made love for the first time. It was marvelous. He was totally open, at ease, and loving. I was too. We were both so thrilled to have found each other, to be enjoying sex with each other, in whatever forms it took, including sometimes simply cuddling up on the bed, touching, and being close. I was delighted that I was not self-conscious about my eighty-year-old body. We laughed a lot as we sought comfortable positions for our aged joints. It had been quite a few years since either of us had made love. I felt my second chakra ignite and actually pulsate. I thought that spigot had dried up years ago. Was there an emoji for that?

After a couple of hours of loving closeness and pleasure, we took a bagel break. Then we went back upstairs for more. Jonah had us look in the mirror together, admiring how wonderful we looked together as a couple. He thought I was beautiful, even with my clothes off.

I never expected to connect so deeply with a man at age eighty. That was three years ago. What I really didn't see coming was that the sex got hotter and hotter. Orgasms were not the old "one big shot and it's over" variety. The passionate closeness and pleasure we shared were charged and continuous, like the dancing hearts emoji.

THE END

ABOUT THE EDITORS

MARNI FREEDMAN

Marni Freedman is a screenwriter, playwright, award-winning author, writing coach, co-founder, and Director of Programming for the San Diego Writers Festival. Her play "Two Goldsteins on Acid" was made into the film, "Playing Mona Lisa." Marni's one-person show, "A Jewish Joke," was produced off-Broadway in 2018. She is an editor of *Shaking the Tree: brazen. short. memoir.* Marni has two award-winning books, *7 Essential Writing Tools* and *Permission to Roar: For Female Thought Leaders Ready to Write their Book.* You can find Marni at Marnifreedman.com, a writing hub to help writers find their authentic voice.

TRACY J. JONES

Tracy J. Jones is a professional content writer, editor, and writing coach. She's co-runs the San Diego Memoir Showcase and co-edits the Showcase anthology, *Shaking the Tree: brazen. short. memoir.* Tracy runs several R&C groups, teaches at San Diego Writers, Ink, and hosts the San Diego Writers Festival/Warwick's Book Club. She can be reached at tjjones1@gmail.com.

SPECIAL THANKS

Jeniffer Thompson and her team at Monkey C Media for our beautiful cover and overall design. Erin Willard for copy editing the manuscript. Stephanie Thompson for proofreading the manuscript. The entire San Diego Memoir Writers Association for supporting this project as well as the San Diego Writers Festival. And special thanks to all of our donors and angel supporters who have allowed these stories to be shared with our larger memoir community.

SAN DIEGO

Memoir

WRITERS ASSOC.

ARE YOU A MEMOIRIST?

The San Diego Memoir Writers Association is a community of writers committed to the art and craft of memoir writing. Our purpose is to create a community of inspired, informed, and nurtured memorists. We host monthly member meetings with speakers who educate our writers on both the craft and business of memoir writing, present an annual Memoir Showcase where five-page pieces are professionally performed on stage, and support the San Diego Writers Festival. Writers of all levels and from all locations are welcome and encouraged to join us to help build their own writing tribe.

Follow us!
www.sdmwa.org
Facebook: www.facebook.com/groups/sdmemoirwriters
Twitter: @SD_MWA
Instagram: @sdmwa

Also check out:
www.SanDiegoWritersFestival.com

Winner of the 13th Annual
National Indie Excellence Award
for an Anthology

Shaking the Tree: brazen. short. memoir.
(Volume 1)

The Memoir Showcase is proud to present a selection of our most compelling true stories, drawn from our annual content. These pivotal portraits speak to our diverse community and its willingness to share the most challenging, awe-inspiring moments that make up the human experience. From a life-changing moment with a Maasai warrior to a wild and unexpected coming-of-age tale in a carnival, *Shaking the Tree* reveals moments of courage, humor, and vulnerability. The stories within these pages are breathtaking.

You can't make this stuff up.

CONTRIBUTORS:

Mahshid Fashandi Hager
Anastasia Zadeik
John Cunningham
Judy Reeves
Kelly Hudson
Shawna Rawlinson
Elizabeth Oppen Eshoo
Cherie Kephart
Laura L. Engel
Barbara Huntington
Natalie Freedman
Donna Jose
Kathleen Holstad Pease
KM McNeel
Richard Farrell

Philip Pressel
Marijke McCandless
Sara Mohtashamipour
Ruth Laugesen
Danielle B. Baldwin
Leslie Johansen Nack
Catherine Spearnak
Steve Montgomery
Sarah Vosburgh
Ilene Hubbs
Kristen Balelo
Nancy G. Villalobos
Dilia Wood
Tracy J. Jones

Available at amazon.com, barnesandnoble.com, and indiebound.org.

Shaking the Tree: brazen. short. memoir. (Volume 2)

The San Diego Memoir Writers Association is honored to present the second volume of compelling true stories drawn from our annual Memoir Showcase contest. This year's winning selections addressed the theme of "Things We Don't Talk About," and our writers bravely answered the call to share the most intimate narratives of their lives.

The authors take on bold issues such as hidden racism, physical and sexual abuse, illicit affairs, the tragic loss of a child or parent, secret family members, and the painfully awkward experiences of adolescent first love. Sometimes hilarious, sometimes terrifying or mysterious, the stories within these pages challenge us to check our assumptions, seek out understanding, and connect with the triumphant bravery it takes to shine a light on our secrets.

You can't make this stuff up.

CONTRIBUTORS:

Elise Kim Prosser PhD
Krisa Bruemmer
Huda Al-Marashi
Laura L. Engel
Lauren Halsted
CJ Elliott
Lenore Greiner
Donna L. Jose
James Roberts
Bill Peters
Nancy "Pants" Johnson
Kimberly Joy
Misha Luz
Amanda Byzak
Katya McLane
Patricia Geist-Martin

Lynn Gahman
Marilyn Woods
Janice Alper
Marijke McCandless
Heather M. Berberet
Sarah Vosburgh
Laura May
Susan F. Keith
Caroline Gilman
Saadia Ali Esmail
MarDestinee C. Perez
John Cunningham
Laura Jaye
Madonna Treadway
Melissa Bloom

CPSIA information can be obtained
at www.ICGtesting.com
Printed in the USA
FSHW012312171021
85535FS